Property of

D1495629

HOW TO PROFIT
BY REHABILITATING
REAL ESTATE

HOW TO PROFIT BY

Englewood Cliffs, N. J.

REHABILITATING
REAL ESTATE

Mary Warren Geer

PRENTICE-HALL, INC., 1957

PREFACE

Certainly, we are all interested in the stories of real estate people who have ventured and gained by improving tired old property. Why, then, a book on how to profit from this activity? It's obvious that thousands of us already know.

The reason is simple. Most of the stories we read indicate that the broker or salesman in question had a substantial amount of money to put into the venture. By and large, most real estate people just don't happen to have a sizable chunk of money lying idle for such an undertaking.

If you, personally, have funds with which to buy property for this purpose, then the ideas and procedures in this book will enable you to profit greatly. More important, these same ideas and procedures will enable you to start right now, without benefit of capital or crystal ball, to earn money on the rehabilitation you instigate.

Our communities throughout the nation would blossom brightly if all the real estate people became interested in helping their neighbors make the right kind of improvements to their property. But to do this constantly, just as a community service, would demand more time and effort than most real estate offices could afford. So most offices are content to pat the back of the fellow who does demonstrate to the community what *can* be done with older property. They admire his initiative, admit the financial success of the project, then forget it and go on about their business.

This has been a normal and natural reaction to rehabilitation activity during the brisk and busy seller's market we have been serving. But there is a general understanding that the peak of the seller's market may well be past. At sales meetings everywhere you're beginning to hear, "Well, Boys and Girls, we're going to have to start *selling!*"

It's a healthy thing. But it catches the average broker (who, I read recently, is 49 years old and has been in business 9 years) in something of a quandary. Just how *do* you cope with a buyer's market?

This book contains one of the answers, a tremendously important one. Way back in 1931 I cut my real estate teeth on a *real* buyer's market. Over the years I've learned that the procedures that bring results when the chips are down are procedures you can depend on in any market. I've watched them reap fortunes through the years for people all over the nation. And, lest I be carried away with my own ideas, I've checked with such people across the country for the practicality of what you're about to read.

Don't just read this book. Try out what it tells you! Pick one forlorn little property and get somebody busy on it, doing the right things in the right way. You'll wonder why you didn't start making money this way long ago!

M.W.G.

CONTENTS

CONTENTS

viii

CONTENTS

ix

CONTENTS

HOW TO PROFIT
BY REHABILITATING
REAL ESTATE

1. HOW REHABILITATION HAS PAID OFF IN THE PAST 20 YEARS

IF YOU KNOW THE PITFALLS TO avoid, the procedure to employ, the many ways to apply your know-how—and if your eyes are open—you and your clients will profit by rehabilitating real estate!

Rehabilitation is simply making property nice. It isn't very complicated. It certainly isn't new—though it calls for some new approaches today.

It sells more property to more people than booms or low down payments.

It greases the wheels of your deals.

It keeps the community and your meal ticket in a healthy state.

It builds you a lucrative and loyal clientele.

You earn while you learn.

And it's fun.

Revitalizing older property is the biggest source of easy extra income in the United States today. Its raw material is some 60 million used structures and a coming million-plus structures a year. Its machinery is a vast number of people trained in the use of today's streamlined methods and materials. Its future and success is underwritten by

1

a concerted, though still quiet, nationwide activity for community betterment.

While public attention is being focused on the new construction being handled each month, *work is already going on* in hundreds of cities to bring the *old* city up to date and back to life. You may possibly think of it as slum clearance, urban redevelopment—big, impersonal programs. . . .

While your own attention is focused on the difficulty of marketing tired old real estate in competition with new, low-down-payment fringe and beyond housing, and other property, *many* people are already making a lot of money by creating an easy market for older property.

HOW TODAY'S CHANCES FOR REHABILITATION PROFIT WERE BORN

There never has been a time when keeping, or putting, a property in nice condition has failed to be worthwhile. Clean, comfortable, and attractive shelter—whether for home, business, or industry—is both pleasanter to use and more valuable than its dingy or obsolete counterpart.

There have to be good reasons why any special chance to profit on rehabilitation exists today.

Here's the background.

● How Mass Distress Fostered Mass Rehabilitation

Those of you who were handling real estate back in the early thirties share a memory with me. Those were the days when real estate was being foreclosed in wholesale quantities.

A vast uneasiness held every financial institution. The

2

banks and mortgage companies and private individuals who had been holding juicy, short-term loans now held a distressing array of abandoned, unsalable real estate.

Along with the bills that arrived at the office the first of each month, we'd get several envelopes from different holders containing lists of the foreclosed properties. They were pretty long printed lists. Usually a few more properties were added—proof that this wasn't exactly the same list we'd received last month. Disheartening? Yes. There wasn't much incentive to go out to see the property —though of course we did, if only to keep busy.

HOLC came along, and a little flutter of hope ran through the ranks. Maybe this would stem the tide.

Before too long it was clear that HOLC was also having to take over bad debts. Their list was added to the handful that came each month.

Then there was a letter. HOLC was taking certain of its properties off the market for *rehabilitation.* They would notify us when the properties were ready for marketing.

A rather strange sight was soon to be seen here and there all over town. Trucks would pull up and men would get out and start whacking away at shrubbery. Roofers and carpenters and plumbers and tile men and plasterers and painters could be seen busying themselves around the HOLC properties. Gardeners would then come and put in a lawn. Clean, protective, "walking inspection" papers would be laid on the shiny, refinished floors. And finally the listings started to come through.

Brokers, meeting on the street, agreed that prices were stiff. But the down payment . . . 10 per cent. And 1 per cent per month on the balance with low interest.

While some of the sidewalk philosophers scoffed, those properties started to move.

Before very long we were all haunting HOLC for any advance information we might cadge! Almost as quickly, other lending institutions got on the band wagon. So we started haunting them too!

There were lots of "smear" jobs—thick paint over years of accumulated dirt. And lots of honest jobs.

Probably our most successful builder-rehabilitator, Peter Turchon, President of HOMES, Inc. of Boston, Massachusetts, got his real start in those days. Boston bankers called on him and his men to get busy on their holdings. They profited and liked what he did. The groundwork for strong financial backing for his future operations was laid.

Today HOMES, Inc. averages 500 successful operations a year on its own properties which are resold!

Arthur Binns of Philadelphia, ignoring warnings from his friends, started on what was probably the first big-scale private slum-clearance undertaking. He had the daring to take over a large block of industrial slum property at the outskirts of Philadelphia. They were row apartments and flats, extremely shabby, and lacking in most of the basic refinements that spell decent living.

As inexpensively as possible (and in 1937, prices were delightfully low) the filth and rot and dinginess were replaced with cleanliness and soundness and brightness.

Against the best advice these refurbished units were rented, at prices increased to take care of the costs, to the same kind of people who formerly lived there. Incredibly, the property flourished—and Binns made enough money on the deal to go out and continue his unheard-of project. Peter Turchon and Arthur Binns are just two of the many who made fine starts.

Very gradually the wheels of industry began to turn, helped to some degree by the nationwide activity in refurbishing older property.

4

But back then even such encouraging news was guardedly received by most people. It took some time for courage to reassert itself to the point where families would undouble. It took some time for a lot of unemployed people to get back on their feet and save enough money for even a modest down payment.

It took time and *repeated* reassurances for business to trust itself to increase production, hire more workers, and pay higher wages.

And so it took some time for real estate prices to take much of an upswing.

Gradually at first, then with accelerating pace, the rehabilitated properties began to move. Brokers all over town rushed or pushed their often still reluctant buyers to the freshly finished, easy-term properties.

Private owners began to hope once more that *they* could sell!

• How Real Estate People Got Started on Rehabilitation

In dozens of experiences that have been recounted to me there has been one common denominator. Most of the real estate people who began cashing in on rehabilitation started as I did, trying to make an *otherwise impossible* deal!

An owner would call me to see his property. More often than not the property that *had* to be sold was drab. There would be spots on the ceiling—ignored since the roof was fixed. There would be plaster cracks—not necessarily serious, but ugly. The paint in the house would be dirty, or scrubbed to the bare wood in spots. Colors were faded. Furnishings seemed lifeless.

The property might be well located, well built, and well cared-for up to a point. But after several years of virtual

5

neglect or indifference it looked "hard times." It offered no more lift to the viewer than all the rest of the neglected properties.

The owner was used to its former status. A stranger would see only a depressing reflection of depression times.

I'd think of the renovated institutional listings. *They* were the competition then!

"If you want me to sell your property within a reasonable time," I'd tell him, "you'll have to freshen it up. Get rid of those spots on the ceiling! They'll make the buyer feel as though the roof is about to leak anywhere.

"Get some putty or spackle and fill those cracks in the wall! Then tint your patch to match the wall. That way the buyer won't concentrate on the cracks and ignore the otherwise good construction.

"Paint that kitchen and bath!

"Turn the window shades!

"Polish the hardware!

"Wash the curtains!

"Do all the little things you can to make the property look attractive!"

Sometimes I'd drag the pessimistic owner out to see one or more of the renovated properties. (More than once I accepted a check on a renovated property, payable subject to sale of the owner's property!) In a surprising number of cases the little jaunt resulted in complete renovation of the owner's property—and a listing that was easy to sell!

Before too long my services included rehabilitation counsel. It's only a hop and a skip from telling people what to do to helping them do it. They didn't know the good contractors. I did. They didn't trust themselves concerning paints or hardware or colors. I knew what had been effective for other sellers! They didn't have money for renovation. I could usually find it for them.

6

Word got around.

Buyers, as always, wanted something nicer than they could afford.

Possibly because I was something of a freak in those days—a very young woman competing in what was then a man's business—I had *lots* of customers! I seemed to get an unusual number of young people, widows, and old people—the short-of-money people for whom the men didn't take time.

Old, tired, run-down property was the obvious answer to their problem. But they were *nice* people, and we couldn't leave their property in run-down condition. Each one of the people started a pleasant chain of buying, fixing up, and reselling at a profit. And each one firmly believed that only I could serve them—even when they had more cash in the bank than I could make in six months!

It worked beautifully all round. They finally owned exactly what they wanted (and kept on rehabilitating for extra money). I collected an awful lot of easy commissions along the way.

My own experience, at that time strictly in the brokerage end of rehabilitation, was paralleled by other real estate people who soon got involved in other phases. Brokers and contractors would go into partnership for fixing up and selling properties. Syndicates that enabled a number of people with very little money to have a 'piece' of the rehabilitation profit were formed. Real estate people became investors and openly put their properties back in paying condition.

By the start of World War II most of the distress property had changed hands. Because of the fear-filled years of neglect, most of the newly acquired property had undergone at least the necessary minimum of refurbishing. Building had started to get underway and had gained fair momentum.

7

The new colors, new materials, and new styles had impressed a lot of people enough to cause them to modernize their older property. And business, compared with my early days, was brisk.

Then the war broke.

● How an Unexpected Bonus on Rehabilitation Came About

Turnover profit on rehabilitation continued after the war started, but another dividend on rehabilitation was added. The sudden start of rent control caught rentals with their conditions showing. The attractive rentals were frozen at prices that showed a reasonably fair return on the investment (Not that anybody was happy to miss out on the obvious profits that *might* have accrued!). The dingy rentals were also frozen at prices that had originally represented competitive value in terms of desirability. And the shoe pinched mightily.

Subsequent rehabilitation might or might not result in enough increase in rent to justify the expense. And all too quickly good materials for renovation disappeared from the open market. In a great many cases rehabilitation of the income-bearing investment was suspended, except when desperate or prideful tenants took it upon themselves.

● How Owners Began the Business of Rehabilitating

An interesting thing was happening meanwhile. In the face of frozen rents a high percentage of owners decided to keep their properties in as good condition as scarce labor and substitute material would allow. Another high percentage either decided, or were driven, to invest in old,

8

somewhat dilapidated real estate. And they too got busy to make the most of what they had.

Maybe the end result wouldn't stand critical scrutiny, but at least the properties provided shelter and a hedge against inflation.

Time and again these worked-on properties changed hands at amazing profits. A peak was reached at which most owners decided to hold, rather than risk replacement at a comparable figure.

HOW REHABILITATION LOST THE LIMELIGHT

The war was suspended, and construction stared apace. People by the millions bypassed the older property to rush into new, low-down-payment housing close to wonderful jobs in new plants that soon were suffering growing pains.

Somewhat unexpectedly, older properties didn't go into a sudden decline.

The fringes kept bulging with new construction that crept both away from and toward the old centers. And the old centers bulged right along with them. Urban lots were snapped up and loaded with bright new houses and stores and factories. Tired business centers were sparked once again with neon and glass and glamour. Lots of weary old buildings were dolled up for the first time since the mid-twenties. Why not?

But stress was transferred to the new—the outlying—the modern.

New construction meant jobs and material production! After years of war the limelight shifted naturally to the bright and the new. From an eager start construction activity grew to fascinating boom proportions. It took over the imagination of the people and the press, and riveted the attention of the lending institutions to itself.

9

HOW REHABILITATION HAS FARED
DURING THE BUILDING BOOM

Nobody knows better than the real estate man that the boom has *helped* sell older property. People still use older property. They pay strong prices for it. They *need* it just as the automobile buying public needs used cars.

The building boom has, if anything, pointed up the urgency to utilize *good* older property. So much of our property has been allowed to go to seed—whole neighborhoods, whole districts, and even whole communities. So much development was shoddy to begin with, and the toll of time and use have made it deplorable. But even such property is being used and used intensively, by people who must stay within certain geographical or financial limits or who have no other choice.

Because older property *is* being used, intensive rehabilitation has gone on and on *without any fanfare* as such.

"Do it yourself" and the color picture stories in the array of new magazines dealing with fixing up property are merely symptoms of an activity that is just getting into full swing! The *Wall Street Journal*, the *Bankers Monthly*, the *Reader's Digest*, the *National Real Estate and Building Journal* and a sheaf of other eminent publications hint at the possibilities of rehabilitation and tell of cities and people that have ventured and gained.

● Demand for Desirable Used
Property Exceeds Supply

The truth of the matter is, more people want desirable used property than there IS really desirable used property! And in a lot of places they're already beginning to get it.

10

Old mansions are being converted into lush, little apartments. Beat-up, old buildings of flats are being inexpensively made decent again. Old houses are being modernized, provided with income, or converted to business facilities. Old business buildings are being refaced, reinforced, repiped, rewired, air conditioned—brought up to the needs of today's business. And each effort is paying off handsomely.

The man or woman with know-how on rehabilitation has a ready made market!

In hundreds of cases I've reviewed for the purpose of this book I discovered a striking fact: in case after case occupants of rental property have eagerly paid higher rent for the improved facilities! In case after case the rehabilitated single house has sold at a profit *to a neighbor*! In case after case business property—even that lying off the beaten path and idle for a long time—has commanded prices comparable with prices for new property after rehabilitation! In case after case industry has preferred the renovated older property with its built-in locational convenience!

THE OUTLOOK FOR REHABILITATION
IN THE FUTURE

Nobody can say with any positive degree of authority that the particular kind of prosperity we're enjoying today is here to stay, although it looks probable. Certainly we can't slow down to an era such as that of the early thirties, short of unforeseen catastrophe. And certainly the needs of a growing population—estimated to reach 221 million by 1975—will have to be met.

Momentum has already carried us into a bigger, broader, and more complicated real estate *base of operation* than we have ever had before. We're entrenched in a vast program of modern housing of all kinds. We're started on a program of reinforcing our old cities from the inside, out. And much of tomorrow's bigger population is already born!

We haven't yet reached a state of adjustment between the old and the new. We probably never will—because America *keeps on,* even in slow economic cycles, dreaming up and achieving higher living standards!

"Modernizing" property is part of the *constant* machinery for achieving higher living standards.

It has been going on in this country ever since somebody figured out how to let light into a log cabin and still keep it warm.

It won't slow down now that everybody has seen the latest developments.

TEN FACTORS TO YOUR FUTURE SUCCESS
IN REHABILITATION

Continual maintenance and improvement of good property is part and parcel of the city of the future.

The effort you put into rehabilitation can, if you prefer, take all of your time. It will pay you handsomely.

It can take only a small portion of your time and still provide substantially greater earnings than you now enjoy. Once you have mastered the know-how, it calls for no more time and energy than you now spend on gratis 'appraisals' or on your regular brand of client counseling. It is a service you *will* be called on to render.

Properly handled, it provides better prices for your sellers, better buys and more enjoyable use for your buyers, and more and *easier* business for you.

● Here Are Ten Tools That Will Help You Profit

1. Materials and techniques for improving used property are better than ever!   Over the past 20 years, and particularly since World War II, the laboratories and drafting boards of the country have been teeming to produce simple, durable, and appealing equipment and materials both for construction and for reconstruction.
2. A vast construction labor force is trained in use of these new devices.
3. "Do it yourself" is now big business.   It enables a host of people to undertake otherwise prohibitive rehabilitation.
4. The urge toward ownership of *nice* property is growing.
5. Earnings are big and still growing bigger.
6. Financing is easier and better than it has ever been.
7. Good locations usually grow in value.   Some of your town's best locations are stymied by obsolete structures.
8. From the day they are finished, structures constantly grow older and more obsolete.   Yet structures are one of our most durable assets.   They respond to improvement.
9. Urban rehabilitation is here.   The great, big, mass-produced and costly sort of connotation we give it is new.   Its occurrence isn't.

(The idea of *backtracking* to make over old property is also somewhat new.   Up to now our towns have *rushed* to get started, rushed to grow with each new reason, and rushed to leave the old behind!   It's a glorious fact about our country that people have gone lickety-split to get themselves the *best* accommodations that could be had—from

13

inside toilets to central heat and now to modern electrified living.

Each new movement that has extended or elaborated our cities has actually *been* urban rehabilitation! It has been causing property to fit people's higher demands *within the city*. It has built values.

People today are *rushing* to the kind of accommodations that new, often outlying, property offers. So the cities must rush to *backtrack* and meet today's demands *as they have met* the demands of yesterday and before.

It will take some doing. It will make some fortunes. And people all along the way will benefit.)

    10. You, *wherever you are,* are in on the ground floor! You know the trends in your community. You know individual properties and their *comparative* equipment and values. You know more about property in your town than people in any other line of business.

Most important, you know the people in your community and what they need and want!

2. HOW TO GET YOUR BEARINGS ON TODAY'S REHABILITATION SETUP

YOU AND A WHOLE LOT OF PEOPLE probably haven't been thinking about rehabilitating real estate for profit. There are two simple reasons:

1. It hasn't occurred to you that it might be profitable.
2. Or if it has, it doesn't seem likely from a money standpoint.

I've talked to a very wide cross-section of people—owners, brokers, builders, tenants.

"At today's prices?" they say in a louder than usual tone of voice. "Why . . . it would cost as much to fix up an old property as to go out and buy a new one!"

So far as they are concerned, that is that.

Do you know something? They have a good point there. The difference between rehabilitating for profit today and rehabilitating for profit before World War II is cost.

Twenty years ago you could have a nice double garage built for $200 or less. Today you're lucky if you can have it built for $1,000. Back in the old days I had a lot of tile drainboards installed for $35. Today you'd almost auto-

15

matically include a new double sink and garbage disposal installation in the job, and the cost would zoom way up over $300. The common price for painting a five room house used to be between $50 and $85. Base plugs used to cost three-fifty, installed. I won't upset you with any more reminders of the bad old days, except to mention that $150 would usually replace all the old bathroom fixtures.

I'll go along with your anguished reaction to today's rehabilitation costs. Even the professionals do.

PROFITS ARE POSSIBLE DESPITE INCREASED COSTS

But I won't buy the theory as a whole. You won't either if you get really interested in rehabilitating for profit. From one end of the country to the other, *some* brokers and builders and owners *are* profiting greatly on their rehabilitation efforts despite costs.

They are going about it in a businesslike way. The outlay for home remodeling alone for 1956 was estimated to amount to eight to ten billion dollars.[1] That amount of money isn't spent even in boom times without good reason. The good reason is what we're dealing with in this chapter.

When most people are not thinking about rehabilitation, and that much money is in the hopper, there is just one explanation. Most people aren't yet aware of what is going on.

The purpose of this book is to help you *succeed* in your rehabilitation promotion and activity. You'll neither promote nor do rehabilitation work unless you can see good reasons why your efforts will pay off.

Let's look into today's set-up for rehabilitation profit.

---

[1] Figure of 10 billion was estimated by National Contractors and Builders Association at their 1956 convention.

WHY "IT'S CHEAPER TO BUY NEW" DOESN'T APPLY TO REAL ESTATE

"It's cheaper to buy a new one," is a slogan that has been recently applied to everything from houses to blouses.

Repair costs *have* gone up, and the new styles and models of almost every conceivable thing you might buy grow more intriguing all the time. The two-way temptation—to avoid the bother and expense of reclaiming the old and to enjoy the well-advertised advantages of the new—is well nigh irresistible.

Actually an awful lot of things are designed to last only until something better is in production. Remember when grandma used to will her old iron cookstove to grand-daughter? When the parlor rug held the limelight for several generations? When the gist of most popular advertisings was "Built to last a lifetime"?

I'm personally rather glad many present-day things do wear out or break down in some way so that the old replacement parts can't be had. It's the best excuse in the world to get something new and nicer.

But structures are not built to wear out!

"It's cheaper to buy new" doesn't apply to *good* real estate! It doesn't even actually apply to automobiles, around which I believe the idea originated.

In that field of selling they can make the idea stick pretty well. They have the best paper device in the world: automatic and substantial depreciation.

● A Sidelight on the Theory of Quick Depreciation

Here's an interesting sidelight on how hollow the theory can be. Back in 1941 I bought a five year old, good make, deluxe sedan for $375. It's original price, with extras, had been about $1,800 when prices were low. I've kept it around for various purposes—carting Cubs and Girl Scouts, P.T.A. stuff, and teenagers. Last week I found a dealer's card in the front seat. Would I be interested in taking $900 for it in trade on a new car?

Dollar values have changed, of course. But if the car had depreciated to about a fifth of its original price in five years, how could it be worth almost a third of the cost of a new car *years later*?

It's a complicated financial world we do business in today.

You quote the same sort of prices on property that automobile dealers quote on cars. The dollar amount has little relation to the dollar amounts of the past.

● How Structures Weather Depreciation

How would you evaluate Monticello or Grant's Tomb? The Tower of Pisa? The Brooklyn Bridge?

So long as structures are capable of pleasant use by people, they have a value that confounds formal appraisal. You can depreciate in terms of obsolescence and in terms of abuse. You can downgrade an entire neighborhood or district, and in 60 days' time that same property can be rejuvenated to large new value!

Structures are built to last, and, except in cases of drastic neighborhood change or poor concept, they depreciate very slowly. Each new owner starts out fresh on the basis of what he pays for a property.

The "cheaper to buy new" theory wouldn't matter to the real estate broker or salesman if it hadn't been transferred to property. Unfortunately it *has* been transferred to property! Sometimes eagerly and sometimes reluctantly

18

the majority of real estate people have 'bought' the theory.

The belief even that it *might* be "cheaper to buy new" clouds our vision. It weakens our thinking about marketing our real product, used real estate!

Deep down inside many brokers and salesmen really believe their clientele would be money ahead if they owned new property out in the new district.

HOW DO COSTS OF OLD AND NEW PROPERTY COMPARE?

Let's start with the item most brokers handle: a good used house. Let's locate that house in a pleasant neighborhood in town.

The house is fairly nice looking, though not striking in any way. The price is $13,500, with $4,000 down. It contains about 1,400 square feet. It has three bedrooms, a partially tiled bath and a half, a breakfast room, a fireplace, furnace, tile sink, double garage, and a fenced-in yard. (It's a good buy.)

The yard could stand cleaning up. Probably $1,500 worth of work would have to be done to make the property bright and fresh.

Now let's think about the item most builders handle: a good new house. Let's locate this house in a new subdivision several miles out from the center of town. (This is one of a number of tracts that have been developed recently.) The garage partially dominates the front of the house so that outdoor living can be accommodated in the somewhat shallow rear yard. But it's a rather wide house, on a wide lot. The house is low and contains about 1,150 square feet. It has two or three bedrooms and an all-purpose room that serves as den, laundry room, dining room, and breakfast room and that is open to the kitchen. The price is $14,950, with FHA terms.

This house also has a furnace and a bath and a half.

The big bath combines tub and shower in an oversize step-down shower arrangement, a possible work saver. The oven is built in. The sink or stove top may rest on an island between the kitchen and the family room. In place of a fireplace there is often a big glass door that opens to the rear yard.

The house is light, bright, colorful, and ready to move into. Streets are in, and electricity and water. There are neat new hydrants for a hose, front and rear, and three nice little shrubs under the front window. Otherwise the yard is bare. The new owner can fix it up exactly the way he wants it.

It is easy to see that it would cost $15,000 to buy and put the older house in good shape, and it would still be an older house. The shiny new one *is* in shape, maintenance free for a while, at $14,950 on a low down payment basis.

LET'S COMPARE WHAT THE BUYERS OF OLD AND NEW PROPERTY BUY

The buyer of the older house buys a home in an older neighborhood where he can know in advance just about who his neighbors will be. He can see how the neighbors take care of their property. He can find out what they do for a living. He can learn exactly where schools, markets, service establishments, and transportation exist in relation to his property.

The buyer of the older house buys a bigger house. It is more heavily constructed. It has certain features or earmarks of effort toward quality that lower building costs permitted.

The property is landscaped and fenced.

It has suffered its initial settling. Any 'bugs' in the orig-

20

inal construction have been corrected, eliminated, or allowed to do their full damage. He knows the whole story of construction.

The buyer of the older house buys existing conveniences. All the necessary utilities are probably installed and paid for. The property is somewhat safeguarded by zoning. The police and fire departments are at hand. The schools are in settled operation. The shopping facilities are geared to the needs of the population and to the prices they prefer to pay. The bus and transportation service is scheduled.

The buyer of the older house is not obliged to improve the property until he is ready. It is comfortable and usable even when it needs refurbishing.

He'll have made a relatively heavy down payment, and he'll have to pay off the balance in not more, and usually less, than 20 years. This is rough, but it saves many hundreds of dollars in interest.

He buys a house with a lower appraised value.

● Now Let's See What the New House Buyer Buys

The buyer of a new house often buys an unknown set of neighbors who may or may not keep up their properties, and who may or may not prove congenial. (When tract offices are selling 50 houses in a single day, how can you tell?)

Markets, service establishments, and transportation may or may not be really convenient either now or in the near future, though the developers do their best. He, like all his neighbors in the new districts, will depend primarily on his car. Unless he has two cars his wife will often be 'stranded' during the day. So along with his new house

21

he usually has to buy another car. He and his neighbors live in about as intimate a traffic jam as the people down town.

On a dollar basis the buyer of the new house buys a smaller house. Although there are good arguments in favor of having less space to care for, the smaller rooms generally demand a further expenditure. Furniture built for older style property just doesn't 'go' in the new houses. It takes up too much space. It looks awkward, old, and uninteresting in the plain bright new settings. The market for his perfectly good older furniture is poor. The price for new furniture designed to fit new houses is high. But he wants everything right, so as soon as he can manage, he usually buys new furniture.

The buyer of the new house buys an unseasoned house. No matter how beautifully built it may be, it will start to show signs of snuggling down into its base. Most new property requires touching up, sometimes complete refinishing, within two or three years. This in no way affects the comfort and convenience of the property. It does stir the pride of the new owner of the new property. More often than not he feels impelled to freshen the property, add to its charm, and mend or mask its flaws.

The buyer of new property often buys insufficient conveniences.

It is not uncommon to have to wait for and pay for phone installations when the lines are finally brought to the new tract.

It is rather common to face a future sewer assessment.

Flood control problems beset many new tracts.

Adequate street lights are the exception rather than the rule.

Major street and highway developments may or may not hit the district.

Then there will be school bonds, first for the elementary schools, then for secondary schools.

Fire and police protection, public health conveniences, protective planning and zoning arrangements may or may not serve the new district in ample measure. If they do not, the tax bill will have to rise to provide or improve them.

The matter of public, mass transportation may not even occur to the buyer of the new house in the new tract. Yet in the not too distant future he may need it most of all.

Meanwhile he can plant and fence his property and pay taxes on the valuation at today's building costs.

● How the Costs of Old and New Property Compare

Please don't jump to the conclusion that I am not 100 per cent *in favor* of new districts and new construction styles! I'll admit that I may have exaggerated a bit about both old and new houses.

Actually much new construction and many of the new developments we have today far surpass anything people have enjoyed before! Both as brokers and as citizens of the community, we'd be stupid not to glory in every good thing about them.

In dollars and cents the story of old versus new properties hasn't changed, however. It still costs appreciably more to buy and use new property than it does to buy and use older property.

New property has always called for an upgrading of the owner's standards. Today it often calls for eventual upgrading of the property itself! There hasn't yet been time or money to equip most of the new districts with all of the costly services people now demand.

While the initial cost of moving into new property is

23

usually less than the cost of moving into older property, the payments are both larger and payable for a considerably longer time—often half again as long.

One can have nothing but admiration for the optimism and nerve of the young families who are flocking to the new districts to raise their families. Many of them know the total cost they're assuming. A lot of them are just finding out.

They came to the real estate people and tried to find something nice in older property they could more easily afford. We made no great effort to serve them. We simply didn't have enough of the modern, competitive sort of thing that appeals to people of moderate means.

WHY MOST OLDER PROPERTY DOESN'T COMPETE WITH NEW

Up until recently—and perhaps this will sound naive to my elders—there has been a state of "no contest" between the old and the new parts of town.

The biggest values were in the heart of the downtown business district. New developments were simply a sign of progress for the city proper. As fast as some of the fairly prosperous crowd moved away from the old neighborhood into the new neighborhood, the old neighborhood filled up again.

The type of occupants attracted was comparable with the desirability of the neighborhoods. In other words, certain people moved out of the old 'best' section into the new 'best' section. Then people from the next-to-the-best old section moved into the former best section, and so on.

This was fine, except that it left the least desirable of the older properties wide open. As the business and industry of the city proper grew, a lot of strangers, or people

24

from across the tracks, edged in to occupy the recently vacated worst old property.

This didn't bother the owners of the worst old property too much. They actually could get more dollar return by loading their property up with lots of people at pretty strong rents than they could have gotten out of a cash sale. And meanwhile they could sit tight and wait for the old land value to increase as the city proper grew.

Cities need workers, so it was sound thinking, up to a point.

Then along came some progress to pull the props out from under their complacency. Many of them don't even realize that the props are gone as yet. All of a sudden it was no longer vital that ALL the business and industry and workers locate in the city proper!

● Three Facts That Have Slowed Your City Down

The old established city is still the center of things, but:

1. A tremendous amount of industry and business has already found it convenient to establish itself a good distance from the heart of the old city proper.
2. A tremendous number of people have found it possible to live in new, up-to-the-minute, outlying property for only a certain amount per month more than they paid for less desirable accommodations in town.
3. Business goes where people are. Every city of any size now has perimeter-and-beyond business centers that have already made the downtown merchants nervous and impulsive.

These are facts you undoubtedly have noted yourself. The starting point was the early war emergency installations. Power and roads and techniques were developed for them, very often in the comparatively wide open spaces. As the years have gone by you and your clientele have marveled at the way these outlying sections have grown.

They haven't seemed to hurt you. Your town has been thriving too.

HOW NEW CENTERS OF VALUE AFFECT YOUR TOWN

Today's dispersion of industry, people, and business is big. It has moved in, practically full grown, and our cities have had very little to say about it!

There has been a terrific amount of municipal hubbub about this dispersion.

It caught the cities unprepared. Their streets are glutted with cars that belong to people who live and work and pay taxes somewhere else. Their comfortable old city plan and operations program have been knocked into a cocked hat.

Your faith in America is reaffirmed if you watch the city governments scramble to provide parking and roads and attractions to woo the outside business. They want to do the right thing in order to lay a foundation for a prosperous future. They feel almost obliged to avoid the outside problems and headaches. And they are in a quandary. Their planning commission is having a *real* workout!

● Outlying Development Has Pointed Up the Old City's Weaknesses

Despite all of our present existing conveniences and amenities, our cities are crowded! Our early streets were laid out so people could walk to work. Our business dis-

26

tricts were laid out for people on foot. Our early industrial districts were situated near ports or railroad service,
then blocked with worker housing, so workers could walk
to work. Our parks and schools and thoroughfares were
planned for less people than are able to use them today!

Despite the fact that our cities have welcomed and absorbed and equipped each new subdivision within their
borders, they've had to let some things go. They've done
a magnificent job—a job that seems incredible to most of
the world—in meeting the demands and pressures for better things for better living for the better sections of their
jurisdiction. In the interest of municipal economy they
have ignored or postponed attention to districts that don't
pay their own way tax-wise. It has been a practical com-
promise, based in the belief that growth of the city would
lend increasing value to old districts. They know what
should be done to improve these declining sections, but
they've been marking time for a propitious moment.

Now the districts that are overcrowded, underequipped,
poorly serviced, and injudiciously placed are in the limelight. Property owners and government officials alike are
rushing to correct and eliminate the bottlenecks to future
progress.

● Outlying Development Has Highlighted Your City's Importance

The stranger arriving in town for the first time may drive
on through to some place that looks better. Several million families move to new locations each year.

More likely he will pause and look around, to see if he
can't dicker to settle in the heart of things.

The housewife, ready for a shopping spree, may turn

27

out toward the glittering new shopping center. Or she may head downtown, where there's a better selection of merchandise.

The worker hired by the new industry or business at the edge of town may feel he will have to 'margin' a new house miles away. Or he may try to find a more substantial and reasonable accommodation in town.

Your substantial citizens may decide to move out, away from the somewhat seedy old city, to a "protected" neighborhood where everything will age along with its neighbors. Or they may decide to move from a good part of town to a better part of town.

The investor may act on the opinion that your town is advancing or declining.

The lender may slate it for greater or lesser loans in the future.

• Outlying Development Has Given Your City Its First Real Challenge!

During this period of tremendous activity and change our cities *are being judged* in comparison with new areas that have started out with space and freshness that our cities do not have!

HOW YOU FIT INTO TODAY'S PROPERTY DILEMMA

Up to now most of us in the real estate business have had good reason to be complacent about our communities. Particularly during the seller's market of the past 15 years, the property in your town has served you well. It will continue to make a living for a lot of brokers and salesmen.

There will always be people who want and need to live in the city.

Probably most of the brokers and salesmen in your town —and I'm talking about all of them, not just the prominently organized—share a problem. New property on easy terms *is* hitting them squarely in the pocket book. The going is bound to get rougher in the future.

The vast program for new construction for the years to come is geared to meeting future demand. The controls *to prevent over-building* are already in operation.

We are already in a buyer's market! Today your customers have a number of choices—this job or that, older or newer property, this locality or that, this price bracket or that—and they're shopping. With a car they can locate anywhere.

Today's shopper includes just about everybody. People are starting to look for the most for their money. More often than not they confuse or identify more for their money with newness.

Putting it gently, the bulk of older property in your town and mine is extremely good property. Much of it looks, or is, dead on its feet in competition with today's new attractions. It may be sound, well located, and even neat, but it's uninspiring. It's yesterday.

Today's and tomorrow's shopper can pass by it without a second thought—just as shoppers passed up the unbelievably low prices of drab properties during the great Depression.

If you are going to compete for the buyer in today's and tomorrow's market, you are going to have to educate some of your sellers and buyers and reeducate others on getting their money's worth. This starts with finding out for yourself just *how* older property can be made to compete for the buyer's dollars.

29

- **As a Broker or Salesman You Fit into Today's Property Dilemma in One of Two Ways**

    1. You can go on accommodating yourself to business as usual—which means lean months and good ones, a few easy deals and a lot of hard ones. It is the "wait and watch" policy that keeps most real estate people in a modest income bracket. It helps the builders get rich.
    2. Or you can get out and study this sales dilemma for yourself and begin making your efforts competitive!

- **What You Have to Work With on a Buyer's Market**

You have read a lot of words about the nature and scope of your selling problem in tomorrow's market. Please don't believe them just because they're in print.

Go out and see for yourself. Take a big, thorough, open-minded, inquisitive look at YOUR town and its surroundings. Then try to look ahead to more new industries, a million-plus more new dwelling units per year, more outlying business development.

Try to understand how your town *looks* to your sellers and buyers today and how it will look tomorrow.

Find out what your city fathers, your planning commission, your builders, investors, and lenders are thinking and doing.

Then look at your own selling territory again.

You have some positive advantages to work with! Let's review them:

    1. Your town is of compact design. The ability to walk or hop a bus to where one wants to go is precious to people of all ages and stations.

30

2. Your town has comparatively reasonable services and conveniences. The gas or water main in the city street may serve thousands instead of dozens. The Police and Fire Departments are within minutes of availability. The schools are established and flourishing. Health and Safety and Sanitation services are established to handle the concentration of population.

3. Your business district is stocked and extensive.

4. Industry in your town works side by side with other industry or business that contributes to its easy operation.

5. A tremendous amount of money is invested in real estate by people who can protect and are protecting their investment.

6. Your town has an important reason for being exactly where it is. This reason is important to a lot of people.

7. Structures in your town have been in a more or less constant state of change and improvement as changes and improvements have become desirable. They are subject to further change and improvement as demand for improvement grows.

8. People need and want to live in your town.

• What You Have to Contend With on a Buyer's Market

We have hit the highlights of minimum or non-existent down payments and fancy new attractions that lure people away from our offices. Now let's briefly list the obstacles to easy sale of older property.

1. Financing. Exceptionally good and competitive financing now exists for qualified older property. Truly *competitive* financing is on the way. Meanwhile, on property that does not justify alteration to FHA or similar top loan requirements, we must create attractive financing where we can. We'll discuss this in the next chapter.

31

2. Lethargy. Both you and your clientele are accustomed to older property as it stands. It takes a certain amount of "doing" to visualize possibilities. That's what this book is about.
3. Regulations. Creating competitive property through rehabilitation is a business operation, subject to rules (and they're easy ones) which we'll discuss as we go along.

● How Wise Investors Make Their Property Compete

There isn't much fanfare for what the wise owner of older property is doing.

You may have noticed that a number of businesses have quietly arranged offstreet parking for their customers.

You may have read little stories of huge office, commercial, or industrial buildings being expanded, modernized, or improved. Many of them are fairly new buildings. But they're undergoing a metamorphosis. One is installing air conditioning. Another is installing a big expanse of glass for light. This one, in a warm climate, is cutting down on the expanse of south or west facing glass in keeping with today's concept of eliminating heat and glare. The next one is redesigning its interior, making way for modern techniques and equipment or making the occupants more comfortable.

These are pretty expensive undertakings when most good buildings are full and have a waiting list of tenants. Do the owners *need* to make these improvements?

They think so. They are simply taking steps to underwrite future top rents in competition with new structures.

And have you read the rental ads on housing units lately? Some of the old familiar addresses now list automatic washers or garbage disposals, 'open' plans, efficiency kitchens, play areas—or some combination of these. The owners know what people *want!*

Did you know that the big old house on the boulevard is now worth three times as much as it used to be worth, since it was made into a triplex?

Have you looked closely at the houses in your town? People by the tens of thousands are working to keep their properties abreast of the times.

WHERE YOU BELONG IN TODAY'S REHABILITATION SETUP

If you're a *good* broker or salesman you want to be in on the activity that pays off both in friends and in commissions. That activity in today's and tomorrow's vastly more competitive market is *making used property compete* with new in both comfort and dollar value.

You, better than anyone else, can advise your individual buyers and sellers. You can *create* new and real value. You can find and furnish the property and people that provide a rehabilitation profit. You can wake people up— and earn money doing it!

Your place in today's rehabilitation picture is squarely in the middle.

Your *sellers* can't arbitrarily offer a wide lot, a perfect setting for outdoor living, or a brand new structure on easy terms. They *do* have property that offers the plus values of city living.

Neither you nor your sellers can make buyers want dull, drab, or obsolete property. But you *can* offer your listings in bright, modern, economical packaging.

You can make older property bright and attractive, modern and efficient. When you do, you offer a real bargain. And real bargains are easy to sell.

Your buyers are entitled to the best their money will buy.

You can provide them with *more for their money* in older property.   You can help them make it *best*.

You can profit by rehabilitating your own property and set an example.

You can enable *builders and investors* to profit on rehabilitation.

You CAN BE a central figure in the rehabilitation picture today!

3.

HOW TO CREATE
BETTER FINANCING

TODAY'S NEW PICTURE OF WHAT people are doing poses an even *greater* challenge to the real estate man than it does to his city!

Just about everything, except the best values in used property, is offered on a "Buy now—Pay later!" basis. Not only housing. Everything, from a helicopter to a hearing aid. A lot of people are buying things they want just as far as their incomes will stretch!

Despite today's vastly improved financing on used property, a lot of it demands a bigger, fatter down payment than most people have. It's *hard* to sell because the people with enough cash to handle it usually expect something newer or nicer.

It's rather a shame to talk about financing, the subject, perforce, that most real estate people know *best*, before you've had a chance to find out more about rehabilitation for profit.

But unless you understand how businesslike improvement creates better financing on certain of this hard-to-sell older property, much of what you will read ahead will seem somewhat out of focus. You're too conditioned by choice, beautifully improved property that almost invariably *fails* to offer easy terms on the selling price: that wonderful $11,500 property that will only carry a $7,600 loan, for example.

THE TRUTH ABOUT PROFITABLE REHABILITATION

It's extremely easy, from the publicity it receives, to regard the professional rehabilitation "miracle" you read about as the exclusive privilege of big money.

Six or seven figure improvements or neighborhood-wide slum clearance *is* big money business. Few of us are involved in it very often.

Here is the truth.

MOST rehabilitation for profit is achieved in a single, SMALL operation!

It starts out with a cheap but essentially good property—the hard-to-sell *bargain* you run across every now and then.

It proceeds through making that property so nice and so competitive at a stronger price that a profit is automatically included in the new selling or rental price.

In its most businesslike form it carries *strong* financing at a price that exceeds the total costs.

You end up with property that more people *want* and more people can handle. The property is ridiculously easy to sell or rent because it *seems* almost like new at a fraction of the cost!

THE MECHANISM BEHIND CREATING BETTER PRICE AND FINANCING

Let me remind you that this is a mechanism that the

usual real estate operator can use only on occasion. It IS a mechanism you need to understand.

On today's buyers' market it is more important than ever to make full and conscientious use of contracts; sound, second paper, private loan help, and the latest and best provisions of FHA and other subsidized or institutional loans. You know them, and if you're wise, you use them.

I don't need to advise you on these. Nor would I expect you to take my word alone on anything as important as a financial foundation for sure profit on rehabilitation. Any successful rehabilitator can give you good advice. I urge you to quiz one whenever you can for pointers on your local problems.

Few of them work as close to the local real estate man's operation as the giant I have already mentioned: Mr. Peter Turchon, President of HOMES, Inc., of Boston, Massachusetts. HOMES, Inc. rehabilitates local property for sale or rental to local people. It has satisfied more individual people than any private concern in the business over the years since 1925. It operates in one of the most conservative spots in the nation, and has prospered all the way.

Like other experts in their respective fields, Mr. Turchon has been both helpful and gracious in enabling me to bring you dependable information. It is with his permission that I let you in on part of one of his letters to me.

> Adequate financing is important first and last. Encouraging confidence of local bankers in the economic wisdom of modernization is a real part of the broker's selling job.
> MODERNIZATION is the key to creating new and increased value in EXCESS OF COST! It can open the door to more living space for less money. $3,000 spent to bring a house up to date can sometimes add $6,000 to its sale price.

37

Your local banker is an astute, public spirited citizen. He knows that when you convert a tired house into a sparkling, up-to-date home you set an example that is frequently followed by other neighborhood improvement. As nearby home owners follow suit, all the mortgages in the area gain increased security. Such face lifting can retard blight, help home happiness, elevate a community.

That is why enlightened bank men everywhere are taking a more liberal attitude in financing modernized homes.

P.S. New homes now cost $2,000 to $3,000 a room. In most parts of the U.S.A. the newly modernized home (with larger rooms and more closets) can be sold for $1,000 a room. Bankers know this.

● Let's Read Between the Lines of This Turchon Letter

First, financing looks just about the same to a long time professional as it does to us in our real estate offices. You have to offer the lender *something he has reason to believe in.*

Lenders are, or can be taught to be, ready to cooperate.

More interesting, however, is this. As you read a while back, HOMES, Inc. is selling 500 rehabilitated properties a year! This is more property than some real estate people sell in a lifetime. This is rehabilitated, older, *used* property. Property that a short time before was run-down, obsolescent, hard to sell, and hard to finance!

NO property will take a strong loan because you wish it to!

The harder a run-down bargain property is to sell (and there are a world of them the brokers are NOT competing for) the greater the *need* to increase its salability, its value, and its financing through rehabilitation.

38

HOW TO CREATE BOTH SALABILITY
AND STRONGER FINANCING

You and the lender share a long range point of view on any piece of property. This includes what the property *is*, what it *might better be*, and what it *will most likely be* in the future.

Of the three, the future of the property means most to the lender. On most of the older property we submit to him, he anticipates a calculated decline in value. That has been the pattern in the past, and without *reversal* of the trend toward decline, it still is today.

Until this particular property, or close-by property, has given evidence that it *has* reversed the trend, then the property merits only low to average financing.

That's fair enough.

● Let's Watch Creative Improvement
of a Good-bargain Property

Again I'm going to turn to Mr. Turchon's extensive experience and paraphrase several statements he has made.

> New baths and new kitchens, often new fronts, and certainly cleaning up and painting are the obvious minimums in bringing new value to old property.

His city of Boston holds some of the oldest property in the country. Most older cities have considerable property that merits at least this minimum. Every city, including the newest, has property that calls for this or other, equally important, revitalization toward new value.

Especially in the case of strategically located older income property, rehabilitation can cost considerably *more* than the present sale value of the property *and still be*

39

profitable!   NAREB's Build America Better Council can testify to this!

Think what SUBSTANTIAL improvements accomplish!

Visualize the worst of your hard to sell bargain listings modernized in the way Mr. Turchon suggests.

Couldn't you get a much better price for it?   Wouldn't it be easier to sell?

See that property in your mind's eye!

A pretty, modern front.   Good sized rooms.   Sound and substantial structure.   Nice modern kitchen and bath. Clean, uncluttered property, ready to enjoy—with a *moderate* price tag!

Put it to the financing test!

Here is a property nice enough to attract a more particular and more substantial owner or tenant.   It isn't going to *become* unduly obsolete before the loan is paid off.   It's a shot in the arm to other owners and other loans in the neighborhood.   And the loan is geared to medium priced property!

Doesn't this go a long way toward *offsetting* the downgrading effect of surrounding property?

TWO KINDS OF IMPROVEMENT LEAD TOWARD GREATER PROFIT

Real estate people have always encouraged property improvement as a means to preserving or increasing value.

● What We Usually Tell Our Clients

How often have you said: "This is your home.   Make it as sound, as pretty, as enjoyable as you can.   This will help preserve its value.   It will make the property worth more."

Not those exact words, perhaps.   But that meaning.

It is the soundest advice we can give to owners of strong or choice property.

● What We Should Say More Often About Property Improvement

There is still another thing we *should* say to owners of declining or run-down bargain property. It goes like this:

"Your property, this very considerable investment, is at a financial crossroads. It won't carry a big enough loan to furnish easy terms at this time when most buyers for your *kind* of property need or demand easy terms.

"You, personally, can provide those easy terms. Or you can cash the property out at a rock bottom figure.

"OR, you can do a fairly big job of modernization and improvement to give the property a new lease on life. When you do, it is apt to sell for more than the total amount you then have invested in the property. More important, the property will then have *become* eligible for strong financing at the higher price."

Here's the way to make that advice good. Say THIS, too:

"Spend what you have to, but *only* what you have to!"

Suppose, after completing the actual essentials to salability—and these can amount to considerably more than Mr. Turchon's "minimums," the owner gets carried away. He decides, in a burst of enthusiasm for a very modest little place, to aim for perfection. So he installs the latest and best of indirect lighting, some custom made drapes and fittings, and deluxe carpets.

Salable? Oh my, YES! But, unfortunately, those extras do not add one penny to the amount of loan that is obtainable. They *do* add to the price that must be gotten and to the terms of the purchase.

To compete for the *majority* of today's buyers—the peo-

41

ple with minimum down payments—he needs very definitely to do the *essentials* . . . and then STOP!

THE BASE OF OPERATION FOR BUSINESSLIKE PROFIT

Thus far you've had half the story, and a very cheering half at that. *Any* real improvement makes property a better and more valuable investment. *Businesslike* improvement can create both new value and stronger financing.

● The Outside Story of Much Older Property

This older property we've been talking about—this early part of town, or the solid if dingy neighborhood that used to be nice—why, much of it is *good* property!

Some of the older pieces are well cared for. Not the latest thing in style, of course. The structures do not take today's best advantage of the space they occupy. Those curlicued porches, for instance. They were stuck on the front of a house whether it faced the broiling sun or sat practically on the sidewalk.

And oh, the ornamentation! But despite our enthusiasm for today's cost-conscious streamlining, some of it is choice. It fits the proportions of the structure and adds character. Other of it, despite the use of even fine materials, is atrocious, ridiculous, and ruinous to any honest impression of the property's basic adequacy or real usability.

Take a look at the windows. Must be dark as a pocket inside.

All this is evident from the seat of your, or the lender's car. As on most older property, the idea of *profit* seems to be what the acknowledgements call "purely coincidental"!

42

● The Inside Story of Much Older Property

Now set yourself to inspect the interiors of a scattered dozen old properties, again to take a good look at what you see.

You're sure to see what my franker customers call "crummy old" kitchens and service porches and baths. You're apt to see "built-ins" ballooned up to match the proportions of the ladies of the more "elegant" era in construction. In some you'll see rooms designed for the rich to furnish and heat. In others, ever so much smaller, you'll see space divided into two little areas where one big area would serve today's needs better. As often as not the shells of the rooms are a drab hodgepodge of yesterday's and day-before-yesterday's decoration, overlaid with dirt and tars and fumes that have defied the housewife in her fight against poor ventilation. You'll see makeshift patching, or rank neglect.

THE FACTS THAT UNDERWRITE THE NEED TO ACT TOWARD PROFIT

More often than you might imagine you will find more people using a structure than it was designed to accommodate. Families are growing. Such places are the natural habitat of the sofa bed, the cot rigged up in the dining room, and the bunk stuck together on the back porch. But for all that, they're "home" to these people.

PEOPLE, the one necessary ingredient to business, are struggling with "crummy old" baths and kitchens. They're doubling up in cramped quarters. They're dusting, and cramming full, and bumping their shins on monster sized, inadequate built-ins. They're turning on the lights in the

43

daytime because they can't see. They're putting the piano in front of the fireplace, or the refrigerator in the living room, because there's no other place for it. For the most part they no longer use their leisure to sit on the front porch. Instead they *get out* of the surroundings that aggravate them and send the kids to the movies.

Does this cover the field? Of course not!

Many people use older property because they like it! It's clean, and it's comfortable. These people like their neighbors and the conveniences of the location. They already have, or they're building, rich family memories.

A lot of people choose the economy of older property! They are used to it. It could be a lot better. But it *is* what they can afford.

Most people use beat-up old property because they have to!

Despite the particular inconveniences they suffer, they use it because there is no other choice. They could *pay* a certain amount more, but a little more would probably just buy more of the same. They're marking time to pay off the doctor bills, the new furniture, or the baby, before they'll be ready to sell and buy something better or to move to higher priced accommodations. Or, they're dreaming . . . but they're stopped by the loss they expect to take if they sell or trade.

● Let's View the Human Side of the Financing Picture

I don't believe we can have a *clear* perspective on financing unless we think of the way these owners and users of neglected property figure.

Many owners of old property are using yesterday's thoughts!

44

They're waiting for the increase in value that city growth is supposed to bring. They're content enough with their older property and determined not to "make fools of themselves." They're glad they don't *have* to sell. They are aware of, but not alarmed by, the competition of easier terms. Why? Because their property dates back to "real" construction! And, they think, "declining" neighborhoods are slum sections somewhere else.

Many owners are being all too cautious! They figure they're probably in for a loss anyway, so they finance minimum attention to the property's needs. Or, sheepishly, they finance the garbage disposal, the water softener, or the air conditioning *ahead* of decent plumbing or the new roof. Maintaining or improving the status quo is easier than it used to be. Just a few dollars a month. You hardly miss it.

THE FINE LINE BETWEEN PROFIT AND LOSS

All of these owners are flirting with almost certain UN-NECESSARY DEPRECIATION of their most important investment, their property. They need *help in interpreting* today's vast promotion on property improvement.

What kind of help and counsel can we give them?

Help in understanding the *need* to protect their investment. Counsel in realizing the *full* potential of their property.

Lenders *have* been helped to realize that it is the *use and condition* of property, rather than its age, that determines the security of a property loan.

Yet many owners today still *accept* their property as a fixed, unchangeable thing that must stay with the fixed, unchangeable laws of depreciation!

Certainly WE, rather than the salesman of materials and

45

work service, should be ready to guide the owner of property.

The owner who learns to reinforce and recreate the value of his property through making it modern and nice for *today's* use and habits is already at grips with the laws of depreciation. If he learns to give it *new* value, then he's in position to command top dollar price for good value when he sells. Meanwhile he enjoys top use of the property.

Some of these owners cannot be taught. They will accept their limitations and shift to better property when and if they can. You will list their property and, we hope, sell it to someone who *will* develop the full potential!

Most people who own and use older property can be taught! They grasp the possibilities. If new or better use and value can be created, they want to create them! They're willing to invest or borrow any justified amount to protect and enhance their biggest investment.

● The BIG Question about Rehabilitation for Profit

Certainly you cannot, in the routine of daily business, recommend wholesale activity on new kitchens, new baths, new fronts, and extensive overhaul. It just isn't in the cards.

But you are, if you want a growing and enthusiastic clientele, going to recommend such activity where it will *count*.

The one thing the average property owner is NOT sure of is just what a "justified" amount of property improvement IS!

To begin with, he is seldom very sure what his property

46

is worth—what it would bring him if he put it up for sale. He has seen dollars shrink and prices rise. He knows what certain other property owners have gotten for their property. He knows how much he has invested in his property. And that is just about the whole story. When you go to list his property he plays it safe and names a high price— qualify it if you can! Or else he simply leaves it up to you to tell him what the property will bring.

In much the same way he seldom figures the improvements he makes on the property in terms of overall value. If he wants to remodel the kitchen and can afford it, for example, he usually does so with a certain confidence that he will get his money out. We have all heard owners say that their property was worth $358, or $673, more now— that that was what they had just spent on the property; $358 or $673 more than how much? They weren't sure.

Yesterday's improvements were made by the few. They were geared to the owner's wealth and to his pride or vanity.

People who could afford it have in the past and up to today hurried to repattern and reimplement their property for each new type of living.

They piped in gas lights, then ripped out the pipes and wired for electricity. They installed a 'modern' drain for the ice box, then replaced the ice box with one of the first refrigerators. They were the first with an aerial for radio, and with a fancier one for TV. They partitioned the big old kitchen for a breakfast nook and then tore out the nook to create a family room. These changes just skim the surface of keeping right up with the times.

Many other people, unable even to try to "keep up with the Joneses," have lived with the cramped living room (behind the porch they never sit on), the not-enough bedrooms, and all the other decline breeders. It just hasn't seemed necessary. It's *been* necessary. The question of whether improvements were justified or not was purely academic.

Yesterday's improvement pattern is wiped out!

Today financing for value-making improvements is HERE! Justified comforts and conveniences and modernization are within the reach of *any* of your clients.

Only the big question remains: How *much* improvement does the property justify?

TODAY'S NEW REAL ESTATE HORIZON: COUNSEL

I believe that the *informed* real estate man or woman is not only qualified to advise on rehabilitation to preserve or increase value, he's duty bound to offer such advice! (If you feel you need a brush-up on clear-cut everyday appraisal, I suggest you read Earl Teckemeyer's new book, *How to Value Real Estate,* Englewood Cliffs, N. J.: Prentice-Hall, Inc., 1956)

It is stupid from a selling standpoint to hamper both the hard pressed buyer or seller *and our own sales effort* by failing to suggest improvements that will substantiate better value, better financing, and easier sale.

It is stupid to allow our customers, simply through failure to alert and encourage them, to suffer unnecessary and avoidable depreciation on the property we've sold them.

And it is poor economics to *force* people into high cost, easy term property they can't really afford only because of our failure to provide a satisfactory substitute at lower cost!

Financing is available to bring property up to its HIGHEST and BEST use! Our job is to channel as much of that financing as we can to this end.

48

● Our Opportunity and Equipment for Counsel

In the course of time every older property is up for serious consideration. Whatever the reason, we are called on time and again to talk to owners about their property.

Once you know their property you know whether modernization or improvement should be undertaken to insure or prolong the value it has. The better you know the owners and their property, the more accurately you can defend how much and what kind of expenditure this particular property in its particular surroundings and location justifies.

You can make an educated guess at the dollars and cents impact of enclosing the porch to expand the crowded living room or of ripping out a partition or pushing out a wall to modernize the kitchen or service area.

How can you? Because you know what users *want* and *expect* in this kind of property in this location. You know what they will pay for the *degree* of better accommodations they want.

You can also say a flat and unequivocal "no" to expenditures that may be somewhat gratifying to the present owner, but that add nothing to the overall value and salability of the property.

How can you? Because you have seen ineffective, freakish, over-elaborate, or inappropriate "improvements" kill the value and salability of other, similar property.

THE BIG PAYOFF ON CREATING BETTER FINANCING

The rush toward what is newer and better in today's real estate picture has left a lot of good property at the crossroads. This property may be cherished by its owners or occupied for negative reasons.

Property just a shade more desirable will move rather freely, as time goes by, under today's best-ever financing.

But this property is faced downhill.

● Five Dividends from the Good-bargain, Run-down Property

1. At the outset, *instigation* of the improvement can earn you a listing, a sale commission, or both.
2. The buyer or the seller profits. You have a booster.
3. The example of this profitable undertaking inspires others, furnishing you with other easier-to-sell properties.
4. The new value that is created *reinforces* values in this part of your selling territory, makes future financing easier, makes future sales more probable.
5. Finally, such modernized property in *your* hands means sure sale. It offers *more for the money!*

Through the years we have extended ourselves to make already salable property more salable. It's still the wise thing to do.

But making *hard* to sell property readily salable, from time to time as the opportunity presents itself, is even wiser.

Granted, it takes more "doing" than the average sale.

Such listings are usually ours for the asking and ours for the qualifying. They offer the *extra* benefits that our ordinary listings do not.

You have little difficulty selling *any* property, good or bad, at a competitive price and on attractive terms.

Why not develop top-notch bargains that are not only easy to sell, but easy to *buy*?

Businesslike rehabilitation does it!

50

4. HOW TO SELL YOUR CLIENTELE ON REHABILITATION PROFIT

HERE'S SOMETHING THAT SHOULD startle you.

A large number of professional rehabilitators *never go near* a real estate office! Many of you are familiar with the activities of the Build America Better Council of the National Association of Real Estate Boards. You read in National's publications about this office and that that has done a magnificent job of proving that rehabilitation is both practical and profitable. Hundreds of cases.

The fact remains that *most* real estate offices *do not make it a business* to supply the opportunities and ideas for profit in this immense field of activity!

Another large number of active rehabilitators deals with only one or two offices that have proven themselves good sources of eligible property.

It is also true that unless you operate in a large metropolitan area you could starve to death waiting for a professional rehabilitator to come to buy his hardheaded type of buy from you.

Where does this leave you? Right in your own office, dealing with your own clientele.

A large number of your *potential* clientele are either dealing with a specialist in rehabilitation or fumbling in an amateur way. Where do they find these specialists? Through a friend, or out of the phone book, from the classified ads in the big metropolitan papers, or by clipping the coupons in the colored advertisements in a magazine!

You're missing out on a lot of good business for just one reason: people haven't the faintest idea that *you* are interested in making property nicer!

If you doubt this, get some friend of yours, not a real estate operator, to quiz a few dozen strange people about where they'd turn if they wanted to fix up their property. I think you'd find that the great majority of them would think of almost anybody else in the world but their real estate agent.

For that matter, where would *you* go? To the bank? To a builder? To some of the contractors you know? To the lumber yard, or the paint store? To an architect? To a handy-man neighbor?

That's the story of an awful lot of property owners you never get to know.

Is there any special reason why they should turn to *you* when they are ready to sell the renovated property? Is there any way for them to know you could help them find property that would really *respond* to rehabilitation?

Of course not. That's the reason why we have to stop to think about you and your office and your clientele and your community before the mechanics of profitable rehabilitation will do you much good.

It is only the mousetrap that is recognized as better that enjoys the well known fabulous sale. What you know about wise rehabilitation is worthless unless other people know you know it.

THE CORNERSTONE TO SUCCESS: AN INTRIGUING POINT OF VIEW

Let's get one thing straight at the start.   I'm not going to presume to tell you how to run your business.   You can operate out of a slot in the wall of a third-rate building or out of a deluxe suite of offices in the best part of town. You're entitled to your habits, your preferences, and your specialties.   Nobody has a corner on the way you should do business, with the exception of the boys who handle the laws and ethical considerations under which we all do business.

No, I'm going to let your business alone and ask you three simple questions about yourself.   The way you answer them yourself pretty well outlines your future success in rehabilitating property for profit.

● First Question to An Intriguing Point of View: Are You A-L-I-V-E?

Naturally, you're breathing.

I'm talking about something else, something you might most easily recognize if you think of a normal teen-ager. It's a very private sensitivity to everything that goes on around you, a burning urge to try on each new experience for size.   It's good, belly-warming joy when you do something hard or smart or kind.   An ability to melt into complete and utter relaxation (the kind that drives parents frantic when it occurs over the arms of the best furniture) so as to build up steam for the next big, all-consuming experience.   And it's a conviction that there are things about the world that you'll be the first to discover.   It's

53

seeing today as the all-important day, and trying desperately to get past today for tomorrow's even greater promise.

Knock away the awkwardness, the insecurity, the foolhardiness of the teen ager, and you have a *live* adult.

Add the sense of responsibility and direct purpose that later years bring you, and you have a live adult who is going places!

Does this sound 'corny' in a practical business book? I suppose it does. But I know octogenarians with more life and spark than the average business man. And I know business men who might as well be sitting in a rocking chair in a rest home. You do too.

Every one of us starts out in life equipped with raw senses. We all thrill to watch the young explore the world they see and taste and hear and smell and feel and sense. The best of our educational system is dedicated to the development of our capacity to live and learn and move a step ahead of the past.

But somewhere along the way most of us select a rut to be fairly comfortable in. We pull some habits and some ideas firmly around us and to all intents and purposes shut out the world. We look at the world and its doing as spectators, content to comment wryly on what other people are doing. The movies and TV are a case in point. They're wonderful as dessert after a day well spent or as comfort when you're ill. They're soporific if you let them mould and crystallize your outlook.

Being alive means just one thing. It means growing. And you have to *see* and *taste* and *hear* and *smell* and *feel* and *sense* in order to grow. You have to *work off* the disposition to let the world go by! If your rut is deep, the job is difficult. But it's worth it!

When you're growing, you are flexible. You can bend

54

to changing conditions.   You can try out and discover for yourself what people see in the latest fad, the newer trend, the decision to bypass one thing and adopt another.   You can say to yourself, "Egad, *what* do they see in messing up perfectly good food over an open fire, out with the bugs and flies?" and still have a perfectly wonderful time out on somebody's terrace eating the good meal they're so proud to serve.

You can say, "This junk they're throwing up in the new tract is a blot on the landscape."   Then you can go out and watch the little houses going up, watch the people's faces as they move in, and know what it's all about.

You can call your competitor a fool or an eager beaver. But if you follow him around for a week, you'll catch his disease.

Do you look back fondly on the "good old days"?

Was the good in the days or in your eagerness to make the most of them?

If you are not really 'alive,' isn't it about time to recapture that old zest?

The properties you handle today are just as different, just as intriguing to somebody, as the ones you first inspected as an eager beginner.   Can you *know* them from your desk chair or from behind the steering wheel?

The deals that are being made in your general territory are just as big and exciting, perhaps bigger and more exciting—when you let yourself get 'in' on their import, as you once did.

How can you tell if you're alive?   Think.   Do you react *all the way* to the listings you see?   Do you think out *with assurance* exactly how to bring out the merits of a property you like?   Does your whole selling territory stand out in your mind like a delicately contrived jewel, with filigree here, and accents there, with elements that complement each other, and a firm backing that holds it all together? Do you remember with pleasure the perfume of that flowering shrub by the front door of 521? Do you know what should be done about those poor people in 1238? Are you proud of your office—the way it looks and operates? Do you ever feel really romantic?

● Second Question to An Intriguing Point of View: Are You Dissatisfied?

Perhaps that seems like a strange question.

The person who is 'alive' gets a tremendous satisfaction from just living and experiencing all the wonderful and amazing things that happen. But it's pretty unlikely that a person who is completely satisfied with life as he feels it will do much to improve it, either for himself or for other people.

History has it that most of our progress grew from a number of people who set about improving something that didn't satisfy them.

Dissatisfaction with existing conditions is still the motive that impels scientific research. It's still the root of competitive business. It's still the gimmick that causes people to band together for a common goal. And it's still the urge that pushes a very few people to the top of the heap in your business and mine.

Satisfaction is the mattress in a rut. It lets people set their sights on a pretty home, then lets them more or less ignore it until it's no longer pretty. It makes the beginning real estate operator work hard until he hits a certain income bracket, gains certain friends, and works with a certain amount of ease. Then it lets him stay there, asleep to the better income, more friends, more exciting activities he might enjoy.

In this country it's awfully easy to feel satisfied. We live extremely well, to begin with, and we live with a staggering amount of cheerful propaganda.

Have you ever stopped to think why everyone seems to need and want a vacation every year?

Could it be that something inside of them *isn't satisfied* with the dull, comfortable pattern they've chosen to follow?

Most people take vacations to "get away from it all." They want to go away some place where they can *make things happen* that will give them more pleasure than their day to day routine.

They're not really satisfied with life as they live it—they just tell themselves they are for 50 weeks a year. Then for two weeks they "better" themselves.

The man or woman who is *dissatisfied* with the way his job is progressing doesn't want a vacation!

If you doubt this, think of the busiest, most successful people you know. From the President of the United States to the kid selling lemonade to earn a bike, these successful people must be *made* to take a 'break'! They're doing a big, hard, excellent job—and they see ways they can do it better.

If you're satisfied with the grind of competing for "easy pickings" in the real estate business, you're dead!

If you're dissatisfied with the property you're offering, with the prices you're obtaining, with the values you're giving, then you have to do something about it! You have to *make something happen!*

One of the most effective things you can do to scratch that itch of dissatisfaction is to improve the property you handle!

● Third Question To An Intriguing Point Of View: Do You Care About People?

Some of the richest, most alert, most energetic men in the world are friendless. In this day and time the matter of becoming one of the richest men in the world very often involves walking rough-shod over any and every person who stands in the way. Perhaps it always has. The amassing of money for its own sake has always been a rather sterile undertaking.

Yet everybody wants to make more money—if only for the good things it will buy.

Perhaps one in a hundred readers of this book *can* unquestionably become a millionaire (after taxes) through the rehabilitation of real estate. It is a lot easier to amass money through rehabilitation than it is through straight investment, since you create a market as you go.

But I'm very sure that the other 99 of us will never make the grade. We just honestly don't care that much about a million dollars.

I've already mentioned that the most important thing in the minds of the successful, big-time rehabilitators I know is *what they are able to do for the people* who buy and rent their properties. That's the key to the lively, interesting, rewarding and monied success they're enjoying.

Business begins and ends with people. They are the only really necessary part of a real estate deal. The world is rich in land that nobody wants. But land that *people want* has value.

It's an interesting fact that most real estate operators center their attention on *property*. By far the most common method of operation is to secure the very best listings

58

available, then to try to find the people who will want them.

It's equally interesting that most successful builders and rehabilitators center their attention on the plans, conveniences, and gadgets that people want. They don't look primarily *for people to fit the property* they build. *They build property to fit the* people who probably want to buy.

You have probably read and heard a lot about "creative selling." It's a nice, thought-tickling term. Have you ever pursued the thought down to a pinpoint? It's fitting what you have to sell to the exact measurement of one person who needs to buy.

Fitting what you have to sell to the exact measurement of one person who needs to buy. Yes, it bears repetition.

Your stock in trade is *every* existing structure that an owner no longer wants. Every structure. Decrepit, or finished last week. A brand new listing, or one that has been shut up in your files for years. A property you manage, or one you haven't yet inspected.

Nothing on earth but the needs and wishes of the people who contact your office will move even one listing! No matter what fancy techniques are used, people buy because they want to buy. Once you've sold a family a home it wants, sold a business man a business property he wants, or satisfied whatever kind of buyer you have, he's through. Your very best sales efforts on another property won't register on him *until* HE WANTS *something different!*

The hardest kind of selling in the world is trying to make people want something! Billions of dollars are poured into words and pictures and arguments and inducements *directed to a big, unknown audience* every year. You, your family, your clientele, all of us, are promoted, bombarded, and cajoled to make up our minds to *want* something we may not be thinking about. Unless you are a determined recluse you can't avoid a deluge of promotion aimed at everybody in the hope that you will be influenced to want whatever it is.

It's magnificent! Our whole way of life would bog down if salesmen in other lines of selling didn't have that kind of build-up to work from.

But can you imagine anyone needing to be promoted into wanting a home or a place to work?

People *come into* a real estate office almost bursting with private reasons why they want and need a *special* kind of shelter.

That's where the matter of CARING about people comes in.

A few people want exactly what you want to sell. That's where most real estate operators make their living.

More people want something you can't readily supply them. Their wants are just as valid, and just as business-producing, if you can satisfy them. Very often they are of the "champagne appetite" variety; and very often your listings are of the champagne income type. Or perhaps they have money, all right, but they're seemingly impossible to please.

If you care enough about the sometimes trivial, sometimes vital, personal wants of people, you can satisfy them! It may take considerable foot work and brain work. But if you care about people's needs the work doesn't matter.

It may mean digging about to unearth the property that fills the bill as it stands. Certainly you, rather than the customer, should make this effort. You are in the business. You know how to go about it. You collect the commission on the sale.

More often it means determining the property that comes *closest,* then seeing to it that the property *is made to become* exactly what the customer wants. Rehabilitation is the means to the end.

DO YOU CARE ABOUT PEOPLE?

People know when you are really trying to help them.
This explains much of your present success or lack of it.

Do you really care about their problems?

The public comes to you. Each individual person is living in a world where people share three big questions.

How does this work? What is it all about? Who will help me?

It's a big, often confusing, sometimes terrifying world. Those questions are deep inside of everybody, from the kid who instinctively loves the teacher who is 'with' him to the hardboiled sales manager trying to whip his crew into action. You can't explain the rise in "how-to", the swing from fiction to fact in the publishing world, or the massive movement back to church in any other way. People are searching.

Most real estate operators are competent in explaining how it all works. They're proficient in giving a smooth version of what it's all about. But only one in a great many gets over to the public the jackpot answer: *"I'm here to help you."*

If *you care* about people's problems they know it.

How? Well, how do *you* know when a salesman is stalling you? How can you tell when he's trying to get you to take something you don't really want? How do you feel when he takes up your time making a pitch on something different from what you asked for?

When people know you are devotedly trying to meet their needs, they stay with you. When you tell them, "This is it," they believe you.

It's odd how caring about people's peculiar needs pays off. You knock yourself out eliminating possibilities for one person. Then half a dozen people appear to grab the properties you've just been considering.

You help one little, short-of-money person, and he sends you business for years.

You start one person on successful rehabilitation, and a dozen more want you to start them.

Is this "casting your bread upon the waters"? "being your brother's keeper"? I don't know. I simply know it works. It doesn't work with everyone. What does? But it will, while it pays off in money, make for more satisfying and easier business and a more loyal clientele. It's being a source of needed help on every possible front because you want to be.

Isn't this what service, the basis on which we earn a living, means? Not a solemn-faced or word-of-mouth interest, but a lively effort to be *'with'* people and *for* them. It's easy if you care.

WHY AN INTRIGUING POINT OF VIEW 'SELLS' REHABILITATION

You have read a lot about being A-L-I-V-E, DISSATIS-FIED, and CARING.

Every one of us is pretty good at one or another or a couple of these states of mind. And certainly nobody could be perfect in any one of them, let alone all three. Any *one* carried to its fullest extent would block out the others. So why all these words?

We're supposedly discussing how people are to know that *you* are interested in making property nicer. The objective is to have them come to you when they need property or counsel or when they want their prettily refurbished property sold.

You already have two practical ways of informing the public of your interest in rehabilitation.

You can run a great big display ad in the paper if you have the money to spare. Of course this calls for backing up your words if somebody answers your ad.

Or you can *tell* people you're interested. Most of them don't really care whether you are or not. But you might whip up an occasional job that way.

Neither of these methods does anything toward rendering you capable of helping people rehabilitate property. And that's where an intriguing point of view comes in.

Understanding successful rehabilitation demands a live, dissatisfied, and caring point of view!

● How This Vital Point of View Helps You Grasp the 'Meat' of Success

Unless your office is already active on promoting and doing rehabilitation work it's safe to assume that your outlook on it is pretty well limited by your other activities.

This means that you need to explore rehabilitation with everything you've got.

Exploring rehabilitation is reasonably dull unless you attack it as an *alive* person would. This calls for unbuckling your everyday habits and ideas and letting rehabilitation *do something to you.* It means, first, going to where the work is going on, getting out of your car, and subjecting yourself to whatever rehabilitation is.

You look with your eyes, smell with your nose, listen with your ears, think with your brain, and feel one way or another about each thing you encounter. You talk to whoever is around to get his ideas. You try to figure out why he's doing what he's doing. You try to imagine who would like what is being done and why he would like it.

You do this over and over again, on old property being renovated and on new property being built. They're related. You get the 'feel' of another field of activity. You get the sense of what is good and what isn't. And you meet the people who do the work.

Before too long you find you have the beginnings of opinions and ideas about rehabilitation work. You're deeply impressed with some of it. More important, you're *dissatisfied* with some of the things you see. In a more or less fumbling way you begin to see how it might be better accomplished. This sends you hurrying back to revaluate your earlier impressions. You begin to want to *make things happen!*

Finally you begin to see *what rehabilitation can do for people.* I don't care how many redecorated places you've shown or sold or how much modernization has taken place in your selling territory. Until *you get in and find out for yourself,* you won't realize what a difference in usability, comfort, and pleasure rehabilitation can accomplish.

The drab, unattractive, lifeless structure offers little more than shelter. Brightened, freshened, and smoothed out here and built up there, it can offer measurably greater comfort, greater convenience, and real pride of ownership. From being something hard to sell it can become property people will *want!* Until *you experience* this assurance of what property rehabilitation does for people, you won't have many people coming to you for counsel. You have to prove its feasibility to yourself, and it isn't always easy.

Much of the renovation work you will see is done on a scale and at a cost that is impractical for you and your clientele. It has been easy for some people, on a boom market, to spend huge sums of money to create bachelor apartments to rent at $100 per month. It has been easy for private owners to spend thousands of dollars changing or developing one style of property into another, more pleasing style. This is the cream of rehabilitation, not the bread and butter sort of activity that fits the average pocketbook.

Much of the rehabilitation work you read about looks deceptively easy and inexpensive. When you set about

YOUR APPROACH TO REHABILITATION

determining actual cost you find it considerably more than most people would choose to spend on old property. This can discourage you unless you see what that expenditure actually accomplishes in a property you might sell.

You might easily see money wasted on some unnecessary but glamourous improvement in one property and discount its worth. In another property that single improvement might spell the difference between an appealing structure and a lacklustre one. But you have to prove it to yourself!

The process of being alive, dissatisfied, and caring as you explore rehabilitation will help you understand how improvements make the difference and it will furnish your proof quickly and easily. Any other point of view will cloud your perceptions.

HOW YOUR APPROACH TO REHABILITATION AFFECTS YOUR CLIENTELE

Once you are enthusiastic over rehabilitation your clients will know it!

You could take the utmost pains to conceal your interest in improving property. You could carefully avoid suggesting that anybody do anything to property.

The very *way* you inspect and show property would generate an interest in improving the properties you know are ripe for improvement!

How does this work?

The moment you recognize what a property *could be,* that property takes on a significance or a value that it didn't have before! It's like being in a crowd of people and recognizing a friend. That property, or that friend, stands out, unique in the crowd. Some sort of relationship exists between you and the property *that other* people sense. Any good poker player will know what I mean.

When you look at or talk about that property you're

'solid'! And do you know something? Your seller or your buyer just has to find out why! Your opinion is 'catching'! Time and again I've had customers *start talking about renovation* long before I've dared bring it up! It's delightful. *They* sold *me* on what rehabilitation would accomplish and how it should be done! Incidentally they sold themselves on the property.

There's just a little bit of larceny in all of us. Usually it's just a sheepish hope that we might get something for nothing.

But when your clients, *or you*, see somebody obviously vibrant and alive, obviously absorbed in something satisfying, and obviously sensitive to the wishes and feelings of the people around him, you immediately decide one of two things. Either he is a 'personality'—an actor or a politician or a very successful businessman—or he's somebody who can do you some good.

When your feelings about rehabilitation cause you to appear that way to a stranger, then *you* are either a personality, or a person whose know-how promises "something for nothing" to your public.

If you are capable of helping them in a sound, practical way then you truly give them something for nothing. And as with every 'give-away', word gets around.

HOW TO SELL YOUR CLIENTELE ON REHABILITATION PROFIT

Most of your clientele are asleep to profitable rehabilitation.

A few of them are both awake and eager.

Despite the vast promotion on fixing up one's property that has been undertaken on a nationwide scale, most people are not of a mind to start. It seems, from the comfortable routine of daily living, to be just another drain on the already taut budget.

How, then, are *you* to get them interested in the possibilities?

There is just one practical way until you yourself are ready to undertake a model project.

Start with the occasional person whose mind is open. It may be a small builder, a handyman, a young couple, an older person with time on his hands, or even a smart investor.

Provide that person with the best and cheapest property available. Arrange the deal to suit his finances. Make sure he can and will carry through. Help him do it. Stay with the person and the property until the profit or the extra measure of enjoyment is attained.

Use that property and the enthusiasm it engenders in its rehabilitator as inspiration and example for the next open-minded person.

Again, follow through. Now you have two examples and two different sources of inspiration.

Learn everything you can from the work you instigate.
Be ready to give even better counsel to the next person.
It's as simple as that.

5. FIVE ESSENTIALS TO REHABILITATION PROFIT

IF YOU WANT TO BECOME PROFICIENT in rehabilitation for profit, an easy method is to regard it as a contest.

Most of the *faux pas* that are committed in the name of rehabilitation happen because one or more of the basic rules have been ignored.

I think I can safely assume that you, as I do, dislike rules as such. So rather than name and defend some arbitrary rules, I'd like to tell you about a successful rehabilitation project that just about covers the field.

It concerns some very good friends of mine at a time when they were using their own particular kind of boot-strap.

The story goes way back to early 1937, and to a pair of newlyweds, John and Margaret.

John *had* managed to see me alone. He had confessed that his money was all tied up in his business line. That the bank said he could borrow $250. And that Margaret hated apartments. She wanted them to have their own little home, no matter what it was. Their own house and yard. (John was in the landscape and gardening supply business. And as John said, Margaret had a good business head on her shoulders.) So with $20 a month which the bank required on the borrowed $250, the payments on the house shouldn't be too high.

"How old is it?" Margaret asked.

"I wouldn't be surprised but what Methuselah finally decided to move into something more modern," I answered. Even in 1937 she couldn't expect miracles.

Her "Oh!" and gasp were quickly followed by, "Maybe quaint?"

"Sorry," I consoled her, "just tired."

At her disappointment I hurried to add, "Listen. It's a pocket size house, with watch-pocket size rooms. The lot is as bare as a billiard table. Two doors away is the neighborhood shopping center. But it's a roof over your heads in a handy location. Surely you can fix it up to suit yourselves. The price is only $1,750. That means that the payments will be $15 a month. With the $20 a month on the loan for the down payment, you should still have money to fix up the property."

They decided to go have a look.

I talked as we drove to the property about the way HOLC and the banks and mortgage companies made perfect little dream homes out of their foreclosures.

"You people fix this house as if you loved it, and probably I can sell it for as much as $2,500—enough to get back your down payment, plus the cost of fixing the place up, plus perhaps a little profit. If you had more cash right now, you could have something nicer right away. But there's no reason why you two and the property can't earn you that cash."

Their first impression of the property brought forth an all-time high in sportsmanship. Margaret chattered about how little furniture it would require, and about how much curtains and five-and-dime knick-knacks could do for it. John silently estimated the front and back yards for seed and fertilizer. Couldn't they tile the sink and put some imitation tile in the bathroom? Not right away, of course. And wouldn't new linoleum do wonders for the kitchen? And wall paper for the other three rooms?

"The house needs a new roof pretty soon," I warned them and, at John's bleakly inquiring look, I added, "It will probably run about thirty-five or forty dollars." John gulped, then looked happier.

From time to time during the next six months Margaret would call me to report on their latest accomplishment and to get some advice on the next step. I remember getting to their house a little before eight one morning. A sleepy-eyed Margaret, bundled in a robe put the coffee pot on and took me on an inspection tour.

Without a single structural change the little house had become almost irresistibly appealing. It sparkled in its new green setting with whiteness and touches of color. The inside had been made cheerful with gleaming tile, polished metal, and starched curtains. Together John and Margaret had made a gay, comfortable home.

Last night, when I talked to her on the phone, comfortably seated in her large, far more expensive home, she said she still loves that little house and drives by it often.

Oh yes, I sold it for them at a healthy profit to my favorite escrow clerk. She wanted a really good buy in something bright and homelike for her widowed father. He needed to be close to a shopping center and not too far from where she lived. (That was pure luck!) And John and Margaret were on their way.

This story, one of dozens from my own experience, *could be your own story* of the proper way to go about rehabilitating for profit!

It contains, with only minor variations, all the elements to success in the rehabilitation you can instigate in the *regular course of your business.*

It typifies the manner in which *you,* personally, *can profit* on rehabilitation you undertake in the right way. It's an everyday, bread-and-butter profit that is obtainable on any market in any community.

Let's break the story down into the five elements that will make even your first undertaking a successful one.

THE "BEFORE AND AFTER" OF PROFITABLE REHABILITATION

What is the background for successful rehabilitation? Where do you start?

Strange as it may seem, you start with a *belief*: that *making property nice* is good for *your* business.

This belief is backed up by four facts:

1. Nice property *is* easier to sell.
2. Nice property means *more value and enjoyment* for your buyers.
3. Even one property that is improved helps your selling territory, and your town, as a whole.
4. It is valuable to your *reputation* and *future* business to build a record of dealing in nice property and of enabling your clientele to have nice property for less.

Perhaps you have never thought of the possibilities of goodwill that accrue to improving used property.

I felt that kind of goodwill immediately after the *first* rehabilitation job I promoted. Friends of the people who had bought and transformed a sad looking little property came in to see if I could find something for *them* to fix up!

Months, then years later, other friends of that first young couple came to me on their advice. And friends of their friends too.

Time and again complete strangers came into our office and said they had heard that we always had *nice* property

71

or that we could help them fix up something they owned.

They were more than half sold on us when they walked in the door. A sale or a good listing usually followed.

I am not even presenting this belief in rehabilitating property as an *essential* to profitable effort. You can be convinced that it is hardly worth spending time on and *still* reap the benefits. But your undertakings and their success will be a hundred times *more* enjoyable and fruitful if you do believe that making property nicer is good for you.

FIRST ESSENTIAL TO PROFITABLE REHABIL-ITATION: A REALLY GOOD BUY!

Getting back to the story of John and Margaret, the house they bought was a really good buy.

How did I know? Because I had proven it to be.

Ours was a small selling office. Our selling territory is large. Our problem was not to be able to show every property on the market, but to be able to show the *best* properties in every price class.

This called for constant and extensive checking and re-checking of every property that even *might* be for sale. It called for knowing enough about each potential listing to qualify it as something we'd be proud to show. And that meant a lot of driving around!

To know all the best listings and to get your share of exclusives on the choicest takes a lot of doing. We sought out and accepted for advertising only such 'exclusive' listings as we believed in ourselves. For me office hours were never long enough. So morning after morning, week after week, month after month, and year after year I 'scouted' our city, long before most of our competitors were abroad. Inside inspection of occupied homes came later in the day—

often in the evening if my owner had requested that I come at that hour.

I had to go inside a property, vacant or occupied, to know every detail about it before I could decide whether it represented the kind of value we wanted to try to sell. All of this effort meant that the properties we showed represented real *value* to the person who could use them. Selling such was easy.

● Price and Value Are Two
Different Things!

Back in my early rental days I discovered the truth of the old saying: "Quality remains long after price is forgotten."

There were literally dozens of rental units fitting any description a prospective tenant might name. Their prices ranged from give-away to high.

Some of the oldest and cheapest properties were every bit as usable and enjoyable as some of the newest and most expensive. Some of the most expensive offered the latest in decor, the most impressive addresses, and the most rigid standards for choice of tenants. Yet many of these expensive properties were less enjoyable, less usable, than their cheaper counterparts. They often stood vacant not because of price, but because of lack of enjoyment value. The quality of pleasurable accommodation they offered was second-rate.

On the other side of the scale were rentals that were, in those days, grossly overpriced in competition with similar units. Some of them possessed an intangible value, a quality that assured almost 100 per cent occupancy even on the worst market.

What has this to do with rehabilitation today?

73

From time to time you'll come across two almost identical structures standing side by side. If both properties were to be put on the market at the same time their prices would undoubtedly almost match. Yet almost invariably one of them would be more valuable than the other *to the person who buys it!*

One might have received better day-to-day care. One might enjoy a better quality of repairs and replacements of things that had called for attention. One might have a better developed lot, with better landscaping and more livability.

One might be flanked by an attractive neighboring property, the other by the kind of eyesore that spoils pleasant use and enjoyment.

One might be shabby with a lot of minor flaws, the other threatened with major costs by a few big items, such as heavy repairs to foundation, framing, roof, heating system, or worn out plumbing.

A difference in both enjoyment value and future maintenance costs can exist between any similar properties.

● The Test of a Good Buy: Detailed Comparison

The 'plodder' is prone to compare his latest listing with similar properties he has known in the past. I'll admit that this is a real temptation, especially when you know the neighborhood and the probable floor plan like the back of your hand.

The test of a listing is how it stacks up in detailed comparison with other *current listings* at the same general price and terms.

The only way *you* can make this test is by *personal* and thoughtful study of every single property your customer might want to see!

DETAILED COMPARISON

By the time John and Margaret came into the office I had the benefit of five years of intensive browsing around through all sorts of listings. The men in the office looked askance at the quantity of pertinent notes I had stuck away in an evergrowing filing case in the back office—the early day rental information (my file card carrying names of both property-owner and tenant, with date) and highly detailed information of each property that I rented.

Many of our sale listings that later came in were those of old friends from my rental file. During the worst years of the depression a great many people rented their own homes as a last resort to forestall foreclosure, moving in with relatives or into a cheap rental in the meantime.

Almost without exception these owners were pitifully anxious that I would find *nice* people, who would take care of their beloved homes. And almost without exception I was able to do that.

In any event, when the owners got back on their feet or got ready to sell, they would usually look me up. I'd make a quick check on the past history of their property for background, for this went on for years.

The current details of the property and the way it compared with other current listings told both the price and value story. Past history only helped define what might need to be done to bring the property up to par.

Every listing we received in any way was bound to possess some peculiar individual advantages that would appeal to somebody. It is vital to know every detail about a property so you can spot these peculiar and individual advantages or disadvantages.

A property that offers a high proportion of individual advantages meets the test of detailed comparison. You can't sell those peculiar advantages unless you *first make* the detailed comparisons! Nor do you want a prospective buyer with you. Successful selling demands that you

75

know both the advantages and the disadvantages *before* showing.

● The Test of a Bargain: How Well It Suits the Customer

Bargain properties run the whole price scale, from mansions or industrial empires to huts or desk space.

People *able to improve* property are to be found in every income bracket.

John and Margaret were young. They had no special talent in any of the building-trades aspects of property, but they were experts in yard development. Moreover, they had the enthusiasm and the energy to tackle and finish a lot of hard physical jobs that improve property without great expense.

For them, this wholesome, somehow cheerful, old four-room box was a better buy than any of a half dozen bigger but less 'different' properties I could have shown them.

So John and Margaret started out with the best buy in town for them! But that is not all.

Rehabilitating that one tiny house caused them to want to do the same thing again on property after property I sold them after that. Not necessarily to live in—for they soon were able to move into a house they wanted to keep —but for the money it made them 'on the side.' And for me there was a commission on every house I sold to them and, after each rehabilitation was accomplished, for them!

You, with your next customer, may be in position to show two properties that fit his exact price and terms requirements. One may be a better buy in dollars and cents, though both are really good properties. The second may offer much more enjoyable use for him. It may actually possess more *real value* to this particular person.

If the customer is interested in improving the property, *he will do a better job* on the property he prefers!

The bargain aspects of a property can be lost during rehabilitation if the owner feels impelled to change the property over to suit his personal taste. They are preserved best when rehabilitation takes advantage of as *much* of the present structure as possible.

If your buyer falls in love with the living room of the less striking 'buy,' you can be sure that living room will blossom under his efforts. Moreover, he'll 'spark' the rest of the structure to match it! He'll create more value in the property that suits him. It will call for less expense, less effort, and he'll do it in less time.

The less striking 'buy' can often be the better bargain.

SECOND ESSENTIAL: A COMFORTABLE COST SETUP

John and Margaret handled their rehabilitation project with complete peace of mind. Neither the purchase nor the renovation presented a burdensome financial problem.

With rather ample rehabilitation funds readily available today, it's a great temptation to show a dilapidated property as a 'cinch' to fix up. Nobody can tell you better than the person who has "bitten off more than he can chew" what a discouraging and disappointing experience this can be.

There are only two ways to bring about a really satisfying and profitable rehabilitation job.

1. Find the person with more than enough money or credit to handle the project. or,
2. Base the entire plan, from ownership to completion of the renovation, on the owner's ability to handle the costs.

77

Either of these alternatives calls for a heart-to-heart talk about the proposed rehabilitation.

To the buyer with more than ample funds you can often suggest a particularly effective way to go about the work or to consider the changes that should be or must be made.

To the buyer who is short of money you can suggest a way to stagger the improvements so that they will not suddenly plunge him into unexpectedly deep debt.

Such a talk before the rehabilitation is undertaken is the very best sort of insurance toward a happy and satisfied customer. You are trying to protect his particular ability to make the property nice and to help him get the *most* from his efforts.

If he is not a professional—and most of our customers are not—he welcomes this guidance.

THIRD ESSENTIAL: A SENSIBLE LOCATION

You, better than most of your clientele, know the penalty for inappropriate action. You have tried to make a loss palatable to the man who has built too fine a structure for its surroundings. And you have seen a cheap and shoddy structure spoil the ultimate desirability of an otherwise fine neighborhood.

A few of your sellers and a few of your buyers are capable of making *unlimited* changes in the property they rehabilitate. They can restore a structure to virtually its original condition. They can erase every identifiable feature and cause it to correspond to a structure being built today. They can make it, as a structure, a dozen times more valuable than it was.

They can lose their shirts if the money is spent in the wrong location!

Part of your service to your sellers and buyers is causing them to do the work they *can* do in the spot where it will do the most good.

Think ahead to the locations where their considerable effort will speed an increase in value. Get them in on the ground floor of future improvement in land value whenever you can. If this is impossible, help them do their rehabilitation work *where people will value its full worth!* They can spearhead other, lesser improvement projects!

● An Important Comment on Location Value

Most of your clients for rehabilitation projects, however, will be small rather than large investors.

For one person who can pay a heavy down payment and command center-of-the-market property there are a host who at best can get together only a few hundred dollars. You have seen this evidenced if you have featured a property for $500 or less down.

The short of cash buyer has a highly practical point of view on location! He may be forced by his job, by the fact that his children are established in a certain school, or by some other personal reason to look for property in a certain general area. Beyond this he is a lot more interested in finding the best possible property for his money.

He is the natural and logical buyer for *variously* located property in need of work, as well as for property that has been improved.

If you keep this great big segment of the public in mind —the people who neither need nor desire the last word in style—your point of view on location will sharpen.

Really good buys in second or third-rate locations provide stepping-stones for the short of cash buyer to the kind of location and property he eventually deserves. In a structure that is properly improved such locations can immediately provide ample, comfortable, efficient, and attractive accommodations.

FOURTH ESSENTIAL: WILLINGNESS TO WORK FOR A SMALL PROFIT

John and Margaret were forced by a drastically slow and rather uncertain market to work for a small profit. Times seemed to be getting better, but you couldn't be too sure.

By dint of hard work and close figuring they spent only $400 on the little house, and with this amount rendered it just about perfect of its kind.

Because the market actually did strengthen during the six months, we were able to get a price of $2,750 for the beautifully, but inexpensively, refurbished property. This was $250 more than the $2,500 price they had been working toward—the highest conceivable resale price in terms of what they planned to do—*at the time they bought* the house.

The important point here is this: by aiming toward a resale price of $2,500 they *had to use the utmost care* in expenditure. Otherwise there was no foreseeable profit.

In their case it actually didn't matter too much. The little house had given them a far pleasanter place to live than a $35 per month apartment would have. A sale at $2,500 with *no* profit would have given them *their own* cash to work with, in lieu of borrowing—as they had on the original $1,750 investment.

Today the need to be willing to work for a small profit is even greater!

The purchase (or sale) price on property is comparatively high. The costs of rehabilitation are comparably heavy. And refurbished property is still in competition with new property!

I'd like to mention again, and this time quote, Peter Turchon, whose long career at successful rehabilitating lends weight to his words. He says, concerning the Realtor's role in rehabilitation:

> . . . . You know where there are run-down, neglected properties in your city or town. You must know at least one contractor who can be encouraged and helped to do this modernization work. Sell him, guide him, help him.
>
> In order to perform a service for the customer to whom you will resell this property, resist the temptation to do too much.
>
> Do the essentials. Keep the cost down. The contractor must be content with a very small profit per job. When he develops more efficiency and builds to volume (provided he gives good value) the profits will then follow.[1]

You may be fortunate enough to find a contractor or builder whom you can interest in making a career of this work. You *will* have a large number of laymen to the building trades who are more than willing to try their hand.

They, even more than the contractor, need to be educated to the idea of a small profit. Their ideas are less tempered by experience. Their knowledge of the unforeseen costs they can run into on old property is infinitely less. If you are to serve them well you need to prepare them for the very *real* price the refurbished property will probably bring.

Then, if they do an exceptionally effective job or if the market stays strong and active, the bonus profit can follow. If not, they will have achieved greater salability within a probable resale figure. Their experience with rehabilitation will have been healthy and encouraging.

---

[1] Peter Turchon, *Rehabilitation as a Business* (Reprinted by NAREB's Institute of Real Estate Management, the Build America Better Council).

FIFTH ESSENTIAL: COMPLETE CONFIDENCE IN A SUCCESSFUL OUTCOME

Every person and everything you encounter hits you with a certain degree of rightness. Your brother salesman may be wildly enthusiastic about a property that strikes you as just average. Without any thought you know you'd like to live in one structure and that you'd be uncomfortable in another one that is quite similar.

In successful rehabilitating everything, the property, the people who are going to do the work, and your reason for promoting the undertaking must be 'right.'

If I hadn't *believed in* the little four room house I would probably have offered John and Margaret something else.

If John and Margaret hadn't actually *liked* it, they couldn't have seen all its possibilities.

If they had been a crotchety, critical couple I'm sure the end of the story would have been far less satisfactory. You, along with every person who undertakes to revitalize older property, need to start with complete confidence in the end result!

In many, many talks with successful professional rehabilitators I've noticed a curious thing. When you ask them what they enjoy most about rehabilitating real estate, they all bear down enthusiastically on the same subject: What a kick they get out of *the customer's happiness.*

Pin them down, and they'll admit to this or that amount of monetary profit. Let them talk, and you'll hear about the wonderful change that took place in the property—and how much it meant to this or that person.

Second to the customer's happiness is their pride in how much more they can offer for the money!

These happy end results are vital to a thriving real estate business. They are as attainable to you in your office as they are to the professional rehabilitator who buys property in wholesale lots and has his own staff of experts to do the work!

These happy results are available to both your clientele and to you, acting as rehabilitators of property you select for the purpose.

They are born in complete confidence in a successful outcome!

THE FOOLPROOF FORMULA FOR PROFITABLE REHABILITATION

This is not 1937, and conditions seem very different from those of depression times. But most of the structures that stood in your town or mine in 1937 are still there in worse or better shape. A lot more have been added.

People buy and rent property for the same reasons they always have. Prices reflect supply and demand and ingenuity as they have done in the past and will continue to do in the future. And the market, in toto, is active.

You deal with one property and one person at a time.

The only difference is that your listings have a lot heavier competition from new property.

The *business principle* for winning business and making money *hasn't* changed. You have to *compete!*

The rehabilitation of used property is your most formidable competitive weapon, just as it was in 1937.

The five essentials we've touched upon in this chapter *are* the foolproof formula for profitable rehabilitation. They are the best yardstick that successful rehabilitators have found.

Here they are once more:

1. A property you *know* is a really good buy for re-habilitation.
2. A comfortable cost set-up.
3. A sensible location for the extent of work being done.
4. Willingness to work for a *small* profit.
5. Complete confidence in a successful outcome *by everyone involved in the undertaking.*

These five essentials are important.

Do they seem familiar? Of course they do. They are very like the elements that enter into every good deal you make!

You can use them with assurance from the first to the last rehabilitation job you instigate. They will carry you through.

Now, with the basis of action in mind, let's move on to the shrewd business of knowing where to look for chances for rehabilitation profit.

HOW CHANCES FOR
6. REHABILITATION PROFIT
DEVELOP FROM THE
SELLER'S SITUATION

PROPERTY UPON WHICH REHABILI-
tation would be both wise and rewarding lies all around
you.

Your and your clients' chances to profit on rehabilitation
are somewhat limited, particularly when you first start out.

This doesn't mean that you won't find all the eligible
property you need to keep both you and your clients busy
for the rest of your lives. It does mean that shabby, run-
down, obsolete property does not, *of itself,* offer rehabilitation profit.

If you were to start out this minute to look for property
that would yield you a rehabilitation profit and ring the
door bells of the first dozen run-down properties you see,
you'd discover what I mean.

Perhaps not one of those properties could be bought in
a manner that would warrant today's costly renovation toward resale at a profit.

Perhaps if you were a professional rehabilitator-builder, able to buy up a whole block of distress property at a substantial cash discount and able to put your own staff of salaried experts to work on that property, the story might be different.

As a broker or private individual, you usually deal with one property and one owner at a time. You have neither massive buying power nor efficient economy methods for improving the property. At the outset you have to confine your efforts more or less to bargain property.

Let's leave this a moment and turn the matter of where your business in rehabilitation is apt to start.

A BIRD'S EYE VIEW OF THE OVER-ALL CHANCES FOR REHABILITATION PROFIT

It is important that you be aware of *all* the places where profit through rehabilitation might be lurking. In your daily operation you serve all sorts of people with all sorts of objectives.

Chances to profit on rehabilitation are everywhere. The big buildings in your Number 1 business block may call for a face-lifting and general overhaul just as truly as your town's most disreputable property. Income and value may be declining on your leading hotel, your biggest income properties, the industry or commercial set-up that feeds your town, your finest homes, and much of the substantial and expensive property that lends dignity and charm to your city.

In a similar way the great bulk of the property you usually handle and, in particular, the run down, almost "junk" property you seldom get a chance to handle may be bringing less and be worth less than it should be.

It would be shortsighted to overlook either the most costly or the most disreputable of your town's property.

There are people who can, and do, work wonders with either kind. Some of the people *you* serve may be the ones these extreme properties fit.

For the most part, however, your clientele consists of the middle income group—the wage earners and retired people. Their ability to participate in rehabilitation for profit may run from a shoestring to substantial investment.

It is sensible to think of this majority of your clientele first.

How do you recognize the right properties and develop chances of profit for them?

CHANCES FOR PROFIT THAT DEVELOP FROM THE SELLER'S SITUATION

Let's reaffirm our first responsibility. We work primarily for the *seller* of real estate!

We are entitled to a commission on the *best obtainable price* for his property on an open market. This means we can't afford to persuade or browbeat a seller into accepting less than his property is worth.

It also means that we can't afford to mislead him with wishful thinking about an unobtainable price just to keep him happy and *get his listing*.

This practice works fairly well in the average brokerage operation because many people decide to sell without an urgent reason. Thus the broker may spend his time and advertising money on a hope of wearing the seller down on price, and the seller may or may not elect to lower his price. Sometime the listing price is eventually obtainable. And occasionally the seller does lower his sights. Quite often the listing office gives up after 60 or 90 days in favor of another office or the property is taken off the market.

This kind of unpredictable dilly-dallying *has no place* in rehabilitation *for profit*.

In looking for chances to profit on the rehabilitation of property we have to look for property at an honest bargain price!

We can very well start by looking for sellers with some sort of urgent problem.

● Seller Situations in Which Profitable Rehabilitation Is Unlikely

In this discussion we are talking about dollar profit— not the priceless and wonderful enjoyment people can get by improving their property.

Fortunately in our American way of life there is lots of room for making property nicer, more comfortable, or more attractive *whether or not* it is strictly the best of business sense to do so. You build the patio, screen in the porch, order a swimming pool, or carpet the floor, *not* for the extra money the property might bring, but because you want to and can!

This very delightful and carefree approach to cost gives us some exceptionally nice properties to sell. It also makes the 'average' price for any kind of property a fairly loose fit. And the average price for any kind of property indirectly takes in the fact that some things besides the bones of the original structure usually have been added. You often mention these things in your ads. So much for the great bulk of property you sell.

Now let's think of most of your sellers.

A great many people sell property after many happy

years of ownership because they no longer want to own and care for property. A great many sell because the present property no longer fits them very well, and selling the property will enable them to buy something that fits them better. Quite a lot of people sell simply in order to buy something newer or nicer. A goodly number sell so they can buy something cheaper or smaller. (I'm thinking here of parents whose children no longer live in the nice big home bought for their background and of businesses starting to spread out.) A certain number sell in order to invest in an entirely different kind of property. Some sell property they've inherited or acquired in some way, perhaps by trade—property they feel they have no use for.

Always they are competing with other average-priced properties of similar kind. It's an even-paced "ought to bring about such-and-such a price within the next 60 days" kind of business.

Some of these properties may be ripe for profitable rehabilitation. We'll talk about them in Chapter 8, "Chances for Profit That Develop from the Make-up of Property."

Your average listing offers comparatively little dollar profit through rehabilitation. The seller who is in no particular hurry to sell or in no dire need of the money from his property usually waits for and gets the most his property will bring. Real estate offers about the best example of free trade that there is. And most of your sales are made to people who are perfectly happy to dress up the property for their own enjoyment. They *receive* the bonus of extra enjoyment and often all or more than the cost of the improvements they have made when they sell.

So what sort of seller situation *does* offer a chance for dollar profit through rehabilitation?

● Seller Situations That Demand a Real Bargain Price

A bargain, cashout, or "steal" price is usually warranted only in an urgent situation. A lot of people do get involved in urgent emergency situations.

Sometimes we can solve their problems by helping them refinance the property, or we can bridge a temporary emergency by rental and better management of the property.

Very often these measures won't solve the problem.

An elderly owner may be sick or helpless and in need of instant expensive removal to some place where care is obtainable. A businessman may be suddenly transferred to a distant city and must have the money from his property quickly to start fresh in the new location. An investor may have a chance to make a strikingly attractive buy with the funds tied up in the present investment property. I won't go on enumerating. You have run into many such urgent situations in your own activities.

When such a situation exists, only a realistic, hurry-up, cash price will meet the seller's needs.

Usually this means a *striking* price—one that will call attention to the property, even on a slow market, *and move it.*

Nine times out of ten, whether *you* participate in it or not, the buyer of the "steal" property fixes it up and enjoys a bonus for the fixing.

The striking cash buy is always a property to consider if your feelers are out for rehabilitation profit. It is available for less than comparable property. *Even without rehabilitation* it can usually be resold for a higher price on somewhat easier terms.

With rehabilitation it will usually *bring more* than the

90

average comparable property! Let's see how this works.

● Resale Profit on Bargain Property With and Without Rehabilitation

One of my early buyers occupied and more or less neglected a six-room stucco bungalow.

Both husband and wife were intent on building up a small business. They succeeded in this and were offered a chance to operate a chain of such businesses in another part of the country.

The husband called me on a Wednesday morning to come to see the property. He needed to leave town the following Friday. Therefore my job was to 'cash out' the property and put it in escrow on Friday, so he could sign the papers and *know* he had money coming when he got back East.

If the property were cleaned and brightened and if I could have had 60 days in which to sell it, I knew it would bring about $5,250. It was drab and dirty, and I had 48 hours—on a slow market.

I asked him to name the very lowest price he would take. He reminded me he had paid $3,950 for it. Then he said I was to get the best possible offer.

I got busy. By Thursday afternoon my car almost knew the way to that property. A dozen people with cash enough to swing it had seen it, and the best offer was $4,000. (I had made a valiant try for $4,500.) My owner was happy to accept the offer. He reminded me that he had had six years' rent for the cost of my commission, $200.

The new owner was one of my regular rehabilitation customers. At that particular time he was tied up with fixing a property I had sold him a few weeks before. The job would take another couple of weeks. He asked me to see what I could get for the property by way of a $1,000 down payment.

Again I got busy. In about ten days I found a couple ready to pay $4,500 for the property as it stood: $1,000 down and $35 a month. The new owner turned it down, but let me show my customers the property he was about through renovating. They were even more delighted with the renovated property, and produced another $500 (which they had held out for fixing up the run down property) to buy it at the same $4,500 price, but with only $30 payments.

The speed with which I was able to turn the property he had just rehabilitated pleased my seller. He told me he would get to work immediately on this second property, and that he'd have me sell it just as soon as it was ready.

He spent about $500, he told me, on the work he did on this second property. When that work was finished, I sold the house for $5,500 to the first family who saw it—a family to whom I had already shown several really striking, but less sparkling properties.

There is one other important thing you might note here.

After my rehabilitator had finished his work on that 'steal' six-room stucco I had sold to him, we were able to refinance it for my buyer at the $5,500 figure, getting all of the rehabilitator's money out of it for another rehabilitation project. This operation would not have been possible on the property without rehabilitation.

● Seller Situations That *Improve* Through a Real Bargain Price

From time to time you have sellers who simply are tired of, or through with, owning property. It may be the growing-older couple whose children are raised and gone away and who now want to travel or live in a hotel. It may be a young person who needs money for an education or income to help along until his business is in stride. It can well be an out-of-town owner, tired of paying maintenance bills for unsatisfactory tenants.

It may be any one of a number of people who need cash *less* than they need income and freedom from the responsibilities of ownership.

Very often the condition of property owned by such people is comparatively poor, and available financing is on the weak side.

Again a bargain price, one that will *move* the property, is indicated. But obtaining cash is not only rather hard (because of the poor condition and low loan potential) but less *important to the seller's well being* than a continuing interest in, and income from, the property.

This is the case in which a trust deed or mortgage in favor of the seller is in order. It is also a case where you can both insure and strengthen his loan and provide a rehabilitation bonus for somebody.

The listing that calls for a low price and a seller-held loan is usually prime for rehabilitation profit!

I hope you will pay particular attention to what I am about to say. This matter of *improving* a seller's situation through a bargain price on his property may be a new idea to you!

Most real estate operators look upon a seller-held loan as a boon to an easier deal. They joyfully congratulate the seller on the interest he will receive on the property he knows so well.

There's nothing wrong with the practice, except for one thing. In many cases they leave the seller with a loan that *nobody else on earth* would consider! In good times, happily, the buyer usually comes through, and the seller finally passes title above a fairly sound loan.

You have an alternative that offers both *rehabilitation*

93

profit and *sound paper* for your seller. Call it creative selling or call it an itch for further business with your seller as well as your buyer *you have an alternative*.

● A Case of Creating Both Profit and Sound Paper

Let's take a property you might be working on right now. We'll say the owner's name is Mrs. Jones. She's a widow.

The property is her old home place, which she has rented to some friends for a good many years since her husband passed away. It's quite an old fashioned place and has grown pretty shabby through the years. She needed every penny of rent for her own use. Now her tenants have moved out, and she has a chance to move into a pleasant boarding house for dignified older ladies. Meanwhile she's staying with her son and daughter-in-law, and everybody is looking forward to a change, though nobody admits it.

On a cash basis, her property wouldn't bring over, say, $4,000. (It's that obsolete and run down, from an investment standpoint.) At the $4,000 cash price it wouldn't take over a $2,000 loan because of its condition.

On terms the property might bring about $5,000—if the down payment was low and the buyers not too particular.

Mrs. Jones, of course, feels that the place is worth at least $5,500. She'd like to sell it for this amount, and she'd like at least $1,500 down. She wants to take a little trip, do something nice for the children, and she could use a few clothes.

Since she's an old friend you agree to try to get this kind of deal for her if it's possible to do so.

It doesn't work out.

94

Finally you find a buyer who will make an offer of $5,000, the chief problem being that he can pay only $500 down.

The bank (or loan company) doesn't share your enthusiasm for the possible deal. They can't seem to find much of a credit rating on the buyers. The property is not their preferred type. They might, just might, venture $1,500. It's tentative, of course, subject to processing.

Do you know what the average operator does? (I've put this problem to a lot of very *good* brokers and salesmen.)

He starts thinking.

What will the buyers think if they find out that $1,500 is the maximum obtainable loan on this $5,000 property?

Suddenly it all comes to him. Of course! Mrs. Jones is a fine little lady. Why shouldn't *she* collect the interest on that $4,500?

It takes some doing, but one can usually convince a nice little old lady about how shrewd it is to have interest coming in. And for her protection—he wants her to know that he has *her* interests at heart—the deal is set up in contract form. This way she won't have the expense of regular foreclosure if, by any *remote* possibility, the people couldn't continue to make their payments.

Does this sound critical?

Perhaps it does. But think of this: Mrs. Jones very probably *is* a nice little old lady.

She ends up with a topheavy loan that *nobody else on earth* would carry! It's dangerous, and unsalable.

An obsolete, run-down property, with a possibly poor credit risk in possession! And Mrs. Jones is *depending* on that $45 a month!

Let's get this straight for the record. There is nothing *finer* than a contract of sale in this kind of difficult situation.   I took pains to point out the efficacy of a contract in *Selling Home Property*.[1]

But there *is* a grand alternative to taking advantage of Mrs. Jones' inexperience!

The alternative starts back with the listing session.

We know, on today's market, that there are two main choices in the sale of obsolete, run-down property.   You can get as much cash as the market will bring—which is usually a comparatively low price.   Or you can sell on very easy terms, and get a stronger price.

No matter how much we'd like to accommodate a friendly owner, we can't effectively price a property too far out of line with available financing.   So we have two straightforward choices to offer, and the second choice, which promises a stronger price, is usually the preferable one.

Let rehabilitation fortify your deal!

Bring it into your sales effort and bring it into your contract!

Get yourself squared away with Mrs. Jones at the start! Tell her: "Mrs. Jones, I hate to tell you this, but your property probably won't bring over $4,000 on today's market, if you must have cash.   If you would like a great many years of income from the property, I'm sure our office can sell it for $5,000, with a *low* down payment.

"I know you will find, if you inquire, that the property won't be eligible for anything near a normal loan from a lending institution because of its age and condition.   So I have a suggestion to make.

"Certainly you don't want to carry a loan that nobody else would consider making on this property.   But you

---

[1] Mary Warren Geer, *Selling Home Property* (New York: Prentice-Hall, Inc., 1951).

know that this is good property. With renovation and normal care it will last for many, many years.

"Let me find a buyer who will agree to improve the property up to a point where a lending institution would be *glad* to make a good sized loan.

"If we sell the property by means of a low down payment to get the higher price, you may have to wait a while for the buyer to make the necessary improvements. After all, if he had more cash he could buy a more modern property.

"But let us find a buyer who *wants* to improve the property and get him to agree to do the necessary work *in the contract of sale.*"

How do *I know* this works? Because I have used it again and again on hard to sell properties.

You seek out the buyer who sees how he can make the property *worth more*. When you find him he is more than happy to sign an agreement with the seller to do the necessary work that will be stipulated in his contract. Sometimes he knows he will continue to be short of money. In this case you stagger the things he agrees to do in the order of their importance. It all ties in with the contract of sale. If he doesn't do the work he has agreed to do, then the property reverts to the seller. If he does, then better financing is to be had when the property warrants it.

What have you accomplished?

You have done two things. You have *improved* the seller's situation by means of a fairly low price and easy terms. You have started on *building security* into the loan paper.

More interesting, you have started a short-of-money buyer on the way to rehabilitating profit.

Perhaps most important of all, you have let rehabilitation bring about an otherwise risky deal!

97

There is one other important thing you might note here.

When your understanding with the seller is that you will undertake to find the right *kind* of person to take over the property, then *you* are in the driver's seat. You are obliged to investigate—even a possible buyer produced by another office. Your specific arrangement for selling the property calls for a buyer who will make the property more desirable and more valuable.

Even if another salesman or office produces the right buyer, *you* are involved directly with the future rehabilitation.

In almost every case that new owner will come to you for future rehabilitation business. You have demonstrated that you know about profitable rehabilitation, and you have shown that you care about the welfare of your clients.

● Seller Situations That Call for More Than a Cashout Price

Have you ever encountered a seller who just wouldn't sign a listing at a price that would move his property?

Who hasn't?

The property may be mediocre and the competition keen. The seller seems to think that *his* property must bring more than the other fellow's.

It's easy to label such a listing "N.G." and shelve it. It can seem like the only sensible thing to do.

When you understand the *extra* price and value that rehabilitation can achieve, it is only common sense to go into the situation more fully.

Why is this seller so determined on an unlikely price?

Nine times out of ten, if you care enough about the

seller's attitude to be curious, you'll learn something that leads to a deal. You'll learn the *real* reason for selling. This real reason defines and determines the possible deal.

The seller who is holding out for an unlikely price may, of course, simply be greedy or unwilling to face the fact that he paid too much for the property. He may be in position to sit back and wait for a possible profit, independent of whether the property sells or not.

Very often the *need* for a greater price is real. The real reason for selling the property is something the seller doesn't always want to make public—a debt that has to be met, a child's education, medical care that calls for a large sum, a relative in trouble. He can very well presume that it has nothing to do with casual negotiations to sell his property.

More often than you might suppose, you can meet that real need through rehabilitation.

The fact that the seller needs money doesn't necessarily mean that he can't increase the salability of his property. His personal credit may be excellent, enabling him to borrow enough money to renovate or convert the property. (We went into the mechanics of this in Chapter 3, "How to Create Better Financing.") Or he may be able to shoestring the improvements, do much of the work himself, and fare equally well.

How do you benefit by instigating and encouraging such effort?

At the outset you achieve a salable listing. Your commission is a little larger than it would have been on a very unlikely sale of the property "as is."

Very often, once the emergency situation is met, the former seller again needs your services—this time as a buyer.

99

And occasionally he becomes intrigued with rehabilitation profit. This brings in money as long as you can keep him busy.

● The Seller Situation Based on Rehabilitation Profit

More people that you might imagine rehabilitate real estate for profit.

Although it is not common, it is not uncommon to run across a property all dressed up for market. Very often the price of the property is fairly high and the seller a stranger. He doesn't call you—you call him. Or perhaps he advertises "Courtesy to Brokers."

He's not especially eager for your help, but he'll pay your commission if you sell the property.

Unless you are *rehabilitation minded* you won't recognize your opportunity.

This man or woman acquires eligible run-down property. He sells bright, appealing property.

And what do you do? Sell property.

I've already told you that many professional rehabilitators never go near a real estate office. Neither do many rehabilitators who don't even consider themselves professionals.

Your chances of selling to this sort of person, or for him, depend on two questions: Do you *have* what he wants to buy? Can you, better than most, sell what *he* rehabilitates?

There is only one way to find the answer to these questions. That is to get to know the professional, or semi-professional, as a person.

Occasionally a professional will tell you bluntly that he isn't interested in working with you. His operation is well

100

under control or perhaps limited by some regulations or authorities. (This is especially true of some of the public rehabilitation projects.)

More often he will talk to you.

Inside of three minutes he knows whether you can do him any good or not. And inside of three minutes you know whether you really want to work with *him*. If he's an honest operator, intent on giving his buyers their money's worth, you usually do.

If you *understand* profitable rehabilitation and *like* whatever this particular person is doing, you're in business! He can usually develop any opportunity you offer him. And you can hurry up and sell his improved properties to enable him to keep on going!

He may be one of your clientele who can do a really good job on the best or the poorest properties in your town. Or he, like you, may concentrate on the center of the market.

If you can satisfy the professional, he can very well put all your spare time or 'lulls' to good use! In developing opportunities for him you automatically qualify real opportunities for your regular clientele.

7. THE DOLLAR-WISE APPROACH TO REHABILI-TATING REAL ESTATE

BEFORE WE MOVE ALONG TO FUR-ther chances for rehabilitation profit, let's do some common-sense thinking about rehabilitation.

Any property can be made more usable, more enjoyable, and at least temporarily more valuable through rehabilitation.

But rehabilitation *accomplishes* more in some properties than it does in others. The increase in value is greater and more lasting. Looking into the future, a combination of circumstances tend to insure a long range maintenance of, or perhaps a further increase in, value.

Although you provide a bonus of satisfaction on every bit of rehabilitation you instigate, you can *do more for* your customer or client on some properties than on others.

Naturally you will have a happier clientele and a bigger and better clientele if your guidance produces better results.

That is what we are going to discuss briefly now: recognizing the characteristics of property that bring about a *strong response* to rehabilitation.

102

FIRST ESSENTIAL TO DOLLAR-WISE REHABIL-
ITATION: GOOD LOCATION

The people who make the most money and get the greatest satisfaction from rehabilitation concentrate their efforts on strong locations.

They may rehabilitate even a condemned structure if it is in a spot where people need, want, or have to be.

They choose locations where people *will* be.

People determine the location value of property.

No wise investor buys a property until he investigates the use to which both the property and the land in the surrounding area is being put. If it's a sound use, a logical use—you might almost say an inevitable use—of the land, then he *knows* what kind of real value the land has.

The wise investor goes even further than this. He tries to determine the use to which the land *must eventually* be put. He makes the same open-minded, all-inclusive survey of the whole area and its surroundings that I have recommended to you from the start. In this way he is often able to anticipate a future *good* location.

This is something you too can do. For example, you may know in advance that the present factory on Railroad Avenue is to be expanded on its own land. If the expansion is extensive, some of the idle land nearby will probably come into use. Some of the already crowded neighboring land will teem with more people than it has heretofore handled. Purchase of either such idle or busy land in advance of the expansion can easily result in an increase in value as more people appear to use the land.

Take another example. A new and much needed high school is voted. Immediately the land within walking distance of its site takes on a new importance to people whose

103

children are in or approaching high school age. It is now worth more to these particular people.

If, through your own foresight, you know that a high school will have to be built to serve a certain area, you could wisely do two things. You could study that area, then talk to Board of Education people about the most logical location for that school. Then you could guide some rehabilitation work into that *general* area *before* prices take the certain jump that the new high school will cause.

Our towns are constantly expanding, contracting, renewing. Good locations become better locations or less good locations. Certainly you cannot take time to keep abreast of *all* the changes or of all the opportunities. You *can* be on the lookout for them.

Even if your town doesn't seem to change, you still have some locations that are better than others.

Concentrate on the locations where people need, want, or have to be. These are *good* locations in your town. They will yield a sounder rehabilitation profit.

SECOND ESSENTIAL TO DOLLAR-WISE
REHABILITATION: GOOD LAND

Some parcels of property in your town's best locations are better than others. They may even carry poorer structures, but they are essentially better property. The thing that distinguishes them is good land.

How do you recognize such a spot?

You recognize it when you stand on a piece of property and let yourself *feel* whether it's a good place to be. For a few moments you forget your office, your next appointment, your sore feet, and just stand there to orient yourself in the surroundings.

Ask yourself *why* people happen to be *here*. Is it because of work opportunities close by? Is it because of special attractions close at hand? Is it because the spot is actually, by way of nature, pleasant?

Those questions do not begin to scratch the surface of the many *local* reasons why certain parts of town are more popular than others. You will know what those questions are in your town.

● How a Resort Town Broker Might Recognize Good Land

Let's imagine your office is in a small beach resort town. You go out to inspect a house on one of the old streets that were laid out and built upon by the earlier settlers, on comparatively level ground above the bluffs facing the ocean, but above and beyond the level beach area on which the business part of your town lies. Most of the surrounding structures are old and rather obsolete in style. Among them are a few that have been either "dolled up" or built new in recent years. A number of the old residents still live in the area.

Your active selling territory is largely in the newer, or later developed, territory adjoining the highways that lead to the beach.

Home property in this older neighborhood is rather hard to turn, partly for the lack of early zoning restrictions. This can mean that nonconforming small houses, even rental units, may be built on any lots now remaining on the market, among and often adjoining some of the stately homes of that earlier day. Almost all of the development of later years, however, has bypassed the older section for the newer and more readily accessible sections of the city on the lower ground and in areas where the development has been more or less uniform.

Now suppose, instead of rushing through this dull new

listing, you stop for a leisurely look-see. You take time to study the floor plan. You observe the condition of the structure. You examine the grounds. And you stand . . . to try to get the *feel* of the property.

This *might* happen to you. You'd be standing there thinking about the reasons there must be for people to keep on living in this old neighborhood, and suddenly, Bingo! *You know* why the old residents haven't moved over to the new district!

This is one of the most delightful spots in town! It's not far out, but handy to the stores and to the beach! The ocean view is *beautiful* from here. You notice a few miles to your left the coast line swings around in a half circle. In the distance, on ground situated exactly as is the ground where you are standing, you can see lovely homes along that same ocean frontage. Farther beyond is the same kind of development, as far as your eye can reach.

It's quiet *here*, despite the in-season buzz and crush of people a few short blocks away.

Why, stop to think of it, the *early* settlers had their choice of all the land behind the beach. They chose this spot!

That sort of thing happened when I first inspected the house that John and Margaret bought.

Mine is a far cry from a beach resort town. It started out as olive or citrus groves and strawberry farms. But when I stood outside the little old house I sensed—quite apart from the handy shopping center and bus—that this *spot* was really a *good* place to be.

Somebody, a long time ago, undoubtedly had looked over the whole territory and chosen this spot on which to build his home. For a home the land 'set' just right to catch the sun and breezes, high above the beds of the drainage streams that once wandered through the lower

106

parts of the groves and sometimes in winter overflowed their banks. It was just a short 'piece' from the old main road—now the main business street of our city.

The house itself was a tall little house, very different from today's charmers. But do you know something? It was the coolest house in summer, the warmest house in winter, and the pleasantest little house on the entire block! I learned this later from John and Margaret and also from subsequent buyers.

The topography of my town is fairly easy to see if you take the time to look. There are foothills on three sides, a watercourse for their drainage running diagonally across town, and a river bed on part of the fourth side.

Five main highways radiate from here, not counting the new freeway.

There is high-lying, virtually level property, and there is canyon or valley property. There is flat land and land that gradually drops to about 200 feet above sea level. There's hillside property and some naturally wooded land in the valleys or lowlands close to the old stream beds.

Now that the city is very solidly built up it is often hard to remember these facts. It wasn't until I first looked at an Engineer's Map at our City Hall, in the course of looking into another matter, that it all fell more or less into place.

Your town may not reveal its topography as obviously as mine. Moreover you may never have reason to consult the kind of map a city engineer works from.

Study a detailed engineering map of your town! Even if you think you *know* every rise and fall of the land, every known or underground watercourse, and every geological aspect of your town, *see it on paper!*

Talk to the people who know about the land in your town! Find a friendly spirit in the engineering or plan-

107

ning or building department. Look up and talk to all the old-timers you can find, especially old-time city officials and old-time builders.

Their perspective on your town is rich with basic information on where values can *be reestablished!* You may run into lots of opinion that can safely be discounted. But you will also run into a paying point of view on *where to look* for permanently good land.

Good land is part of long time value. It is only good sense to capitalize on it.

The *easiest-to-rehabilitate* structure in the world won't develop a long range increment in value if it's on poor land. Sooner or later the hazard that makes it poor land will nibble into the profits, or perhaps devour the whole. Even if you can turn the property fast, you don't want that blame following you.

● How Good Land Helps Insure Rehabilitation Profit

Let's stand off for a moment and take a quick perspective on a city.

People congregate in certain important spots, and cities come into being. Good times come, and cities expand. Slow times come, and cities stop expanding and contract upon themselves.

By and large, the people stay on good land, even when its dollar value declines.

The *less* good land has its ups and downs, but each time it goes down it goes lower in the scale of desirability. Why? Because in the good times in between, more good land has been developed for people to use.

People in your town and mine have stayed on some of

108

the best land until perhaps the bulk of the structures are sadly behind the times.

Today's pressures—the competition from outlying new developments and the resultant congestion in the hearts of most cities—can't be ignored.

You, personally, may have little to do with working out a new pattern for your city's future. But you shouldn't overlook one thing.

The *good land* in your town *will always be put to good use!*

You and your clientele are *safe* in revitalizing structures on good land.

Suppose such a structure is in an area that will unexpectedly be condemned for a new future use? Each parcel of property is condemned at its fair market value. The rehabilitated property automatically carries a higher valuation. And in the meantime your owners have been having the wonderful plus values of better, more enjoyable use.

Suppose on the other hand that future plans for your city call for revitalizing the old section for its original use and purpose. Your buyer or owner will gain the increase in value that comes from improving the neighboring property!

• A Special Comment on Good Land

In most communities the original "lay of the land" determines what is good and what isn't.

In many communities—and yours may be one of them—land has been *made* good for unlimited future use.

Swamp land may have been adequately drained and protected against future water. Shifting land may have been successfully controlled by way of adequate engineer-

109

ing.   Canyon land may have been properly filled.   Water-courses may have been effectively diverted.

It is well worth your while to find out whether such feats have been, or will be, performed in your area.   It is even *more* important to determine whether the reclaimed land *is now good*.

Your Engineering Department can fill you in on what has been done and what is being contemplated.

The structures and the people *using* that land can show you how successful the reclamation was.

Never *assume* that land is either good or bad!

No matter how spectacular an improvement project may be, only *continual satisfactory* use of the land determines its future value.

Find out *for yourself* what the facts and the feel of the land are.

Your most successful rehabilitation projects will take place on good land, whether natural or developed by man. People *choose* and *prefer* the advantages you can *sell* when the land is good.

THIRD ESSENTIAL TO DOLLAR-WISE REHABILITATION: GOOD STRUCTURE

An awful lot of history was written into the books before FHA specifications—or even building codes, for that matter—came into being.   So beyond a certain point in our recollection, good structure depended on the man who did the building.

Fortunately for us today, pride seems to have been prevalent in days past.   A very great number of old structures had enough draftsmanship, craftsmanship, good material, and good intent to keep them standing until today.   Many of them are in full, daily use.

GOOD STRUCTURE

But a happen-so approach to structure has always been normal to some people. So some of the old structures that are in use are in considerably less than sound condition.

This *lack of certainty* about what lies under the surface of an older structure is part and parcel of a lot of rehabilitation possibilities.

If the structure is sound, then almost anyone can, with proper guidance, profit on the effort and material expended on its rehabilitation.

If the structure is *less* than sound, then profitable rehabilitation *starts* with the right kind of attention to what is wrong. This may constitute a large or a small item of cost. In this respect it affects rehabilitation profit.

Real estate men and women are *not,* by virtue of their profession, *experts on construction.* But. . . .

They have more knowledge of construction than the average layman. This stems from their greater than average contact with new construction and with the maintenance and improvement of older property.

Handed a set of blueprints, few of us would feel cocky about handling the whole building job.

Asked to diagnose the nature of the trouble in a fifty year old structure, we'd be at something of a loss. We could probably spot the trouble, but we'd not feel competent to correct the trouble both properly and economically.

Rehabilitation 'takes' best on sound structure. If the structure fails, the rehabilitation falls away and disintegrates with it.

Some of the most effective rehabilitation occurs on the structure that is basically sound, but that is unsound in some particular that feasibly can be corrected.

If you must rebuild a portion of a structure before it can profitably be further rehabilitated, it is vital that the *total* structure is sound enough to justify this extra expense.

111

Let's illustrate this. Suppose you examine an apparently well built home. There has been nice attention to craftsmanship details. The building looks trim and true. But as you walk through the house the floors seem to spring under your tread.

You look down below and see that the floor joists are pretty widely spaced. They run for rather great distances without bracing. Probably there just isn't enough support to make the floors solid.

If you were to install the necessary new cabinet work and cupboards above and make plans for heavy modern washers, dryers, refrigerator, freezer, and possibly the next user's grand piano, the floors just might not take the load.

Here's an item of structure that can run into money to correct. It is, however, something that can be corrected rather easily if all the other aspects of the costs of the deal are satisfactory.

Suppose, though, that you look at a similarly interesting old house. At first glance you are impressed with the quality of the materials that went into the finishing—the woodwork, floors, tile, screens, and such. The floors are good and solid, and the layout attractive.

Inside the house one item catches your eye. There are bad moldy looking patches under most of the windows.

Outside you notice that the roof seems warped and crooked. The covering is in very bad shape. Apparently the original roof is still in service. You didn't notice any spots on the ceilings, but the ceilings could have been recently repainted and the spots obliterated.

That structure quite possibly has suffered from moisture and rot, at least in a considerable, noticeable area.

Correcting this problem may call for a structure-wide job. It may be correctable by piecemeal attack. It all depends on the amount of *concealed* damage.

112

Only *expert* examination of the total structure—no matter how well or elaborately built it was at the start—will reveal whether rehabilitation will yield a dollar profit.

Such examination is in the province of the architect, the building contractor, the licensed appraiser, or the man whose job it is to examine structure for conservative loan purposes.

The architect and the building contractor can detail the proper and economical correction and make a fair estimate of the cost.

Forget your prejudice about people "butting in" on your deals and *seek* the *expert* who can give you an accurate picture of total structural condition. His findings will help identify good construction in a structure that seems faulty. They will help you spot unsound structure in a building that looks pretty good. He will help you think clearly and counsel wisely on the property in question.

If you're in doubt about a structure, get expert advice! It's the dollar-wise thing to do.

FOURTH ESSENTIAL TO DOLLAR-WISE REHABILITATION: ADAPTABILITY

Rehabilitation is profitable only when the *use* of the property is improved. You may renovate a property for the same use or convert it to a different use.

There is great good sense in turning a house into a duplex, subdividing a big store into two or three little ones, making a big one from two or more little ones, or transforming a nondescript structure into classy professional suites . . . spending a large sum to bring out the potential charm and enjoyable use of *any* older building—if the *reason* is a good one!

113

The reason could be strong demand, high rentals, or even just enough prosperity to permit extra luxury.

The *result* of the rehabilitation should be practical in terms of dollars and cents.

There is, of course, no reason in the world why a prosperous person shouldn't rehabilitate his property to become any lovely thing he prefers and can afford. For the average person, this extensive transformation of property just for personal pleasure is usually impractical.

The creating of the desired result needs to lie within an easily realized sale or rental price or within the budget of the rehabilitator.

When you think of rehabilitation from this standpoint you can see that the *property* in question is extremely important. If the property *adapts easily* to the improved or new use, the project will come out better, dollar-wise, than if it doesn't.

We've said before that most people aren't even thinking about profitable rehabilitation. Another fact is even truer.

Most people don't know the difference between shrewd and casual property improvement. They need your wise guidance.

The Joneses, for example, might decide to tackle extremely difficult alterations in their house which is *not* well adapted to conversion to a duplex. They could easily choose a plan for alteration that calls for twice the work and expense necessary to achieve an equally desirable duplex. In doing either of these things they would be *fighting* the existing structure.

Their property, which is not readily adaptable to conversion to a duplex, might be ideally adapted to modernization and improvement as a home, as a home and office, as a store and small apartment, or as a set of bachelor apartments.

A lot of things enter into adaptability. There's location

114

in terms of demand, there's zoning, type of construction, layout, and, of course, the relative costs of doing this or that to the property. We won't elaborate on these things here.

The important thing to keep in mind is this: you are money ahead when you instigate the rehabilitation to which *the whole property is best adapted.*

● Joint Adaptability of Land and Structure

Let's think of this whole property.

If the Jones' house is not in such a hot *spot* for duplexes, then the use to which the *structure* most readily adapts (in accord with existing zoning, of course) dictates the dollar-wise choice of future development.

When you suggest or do rehabilitation work, *go along with the existing property* just as far as you can. See what can be done with *its* features before you decide to super-impose other features. Try to adapt your ideas to the property as it *now* stands. Salvage every bit of value that you can in land, in structure, and in both.

The property that adapts readily to its best future use is a dollar-wise property to rehabilitate.

THE FOUR-WAY TEST FOR DOLLAR-WISE PROPERTY

It is not as hard as you might think to find property that *will* make a strong and lasting response to rehabilitation. Every town holds lots of them.

Take time with the lower priced older listing to deter-mine whether it possesses these four characteristics.

1. A location where people need, want, or have to be.
2. A lot that lies on permanently good land.

115

3. Basically sound total structure.
4. Rather easy adaptability to today's best use, either in land or structure, or in both.

When you come upon a property that encompasses all four of these characteristics, you are 'solid.'

You can offer it, with absolute confidence and assurance, to your town's shrewdest investor or to the next customer who can scrape together a few hundred dollars.

Dollar-wise it is a *good* property for profitable rehabilitation.

As we move along to further chances for profit that develop in the course of your regular business, keep this four way test in mind.

Apply it to property that *might* be ripe for profitable rehabilitation, and it will tell you which properties *are* real profit makers.

Concentrate *your* efforts on the *real* profit makers.

116

8. CHANCES FOR PROFIT THAT DEVELOP FROM THE MAKE-UP OF PROPERTY

A GREAT MANY PROPERTIES JUST stand and wait for someone to improve them and take a profit.

So for now let's make a complete about-face and forget about the price of property. Let's just think about property and the chances it offers for profit through rehabilitation.

In some cases rehabilitation will be so tremendously worth-while that price can be a secondary consideration. If you learn to spot the potential profit that *property* offers, then you will recognize it instantly in the listings you handle.

You will also be alert *to try to control the sale of such* promising property.

More important, you will learn to build into your listings opportunities for profit. You will then furnish the "something for nothing" that people are alert for.

THE FOUR WAYS IN WHICH PROPERTY CAN BE IMPROVED

There are only four things you can do to existing property to improve it.

117

1. You can restore it to "like new" condition.
2. You can make it adapt to a new user or to a new use.
3. You can make it pay better.
4. You can turn it into something entirely different.

Practically every *existing* property can stand some degree of restoration—including the new house that was just occupied last week. People automatically do things to property that need erasing.

Practically every *bargain* property can be profitably adapted to a new user or a new use.

The great bulk of *income* property can be made to pay better.

A fair proportion of the *properties in use* could be *more* useful (and therefore more valuable) if they were used for something else.

That's the sum and substance of the possibilities, and they're listed in the order of occurrence that you'll find in the average office. You have more occasions to see to it that property is restored than you have bargains that can be profitably altered. You usually have less business in selling income property than you do in selling bargains. And in general you sell property to people who will continue to make the same use of the property.

So let's start with the chance for profit that can be found in the great bulk of your listings.

THE MOST COMMON CHANCE FOR PROFIT: RESTORATION

A certain percentage of your listings are in absolutely tip-top shape. You know a buyer can move into them with little thought of maintenance expense in the near future.

A far greater percentage of the property on the market

118

holds no such promise. These properties have suffered from three things: time, use, and some degree of neglect.

This doesn't necessarily mean that most owners fail to fix the roof when it leaks, the faucet when it drips, or panes of glass when they break. It does mean that most owners *assume* that their property is in good shape until they see some evidence that something is wrong. After all, you don't normally go looking for trouble.

Even the property that is periodically checked and repaired against future damage undergoes wear and tear from use. The floors lose some of their original smoothness and luster. Woodwork takes accidental bumps and gouges. Walls are pierced for picture or drapery hooks. Latches grow loose from turning. Pipes fill with rust or by sedimentation. And so on.

While these things are happening, the structure is gradually aging. Of itself it may remain as strong and true as the day it was built. In comparison with newer structures it *seems* older. It becomes somewhat dated by virtue of its particular shape, materials, or architectural features. The areas of current interest (today the kitchen, bath and service area—yesterday the living room and master bedroom)are just short of modern.

So far as the use of the property goes, it is just as good and comfortable as it ever was. Perhaps it offers far better and more comfortable use than its latest competition.

Your town and mine contain a host of such properties. They are good. They are solid. Structures up and down the block and for a few blocks either way, are of about the same general age and character. The people in the area value and pay for the same general sort of accommodation.

You're pleased when you tie up a listing on one of these properties. You have always had pretty good luck on your listings in this neighborhood.

But wait a minute. Property hasn't been turning as well

in this area as it used to. You still like the listing, but you're not as *sure* as you once were of a quick and easy sale. A lot of people to whom you've shown nearby property have turned it down in favor of new housing.

In view of all you have read so far in this book, ask yourself why?

Isn't it because even if it is good property, or perhaps really excellent property, it is still very definitely used property?

● What Restoration Is

Restoration is just what the word implies.

Good restoration means that the floors are like new, the walls smooth and undamaged, the ceilings clean and free of cracks and stains. It means that the plumbing has been inspected and repaired or replaced, if need be, to assure maximum future trouble-free use. It means that the roof and gutters have been made secure against several years' weather. It means that wiring is safe and adequate for normal present day use, that the heating unit or units function well. The whole property looks fresh and unhandled. And it means that everything—windows, latches, drawers, screens, storm windows, and so on—are in first class working order.

● What Restoration Means to Your Buyers

Let's suppose that *you* have just sold your home and have thus become a 'customer' for another one.

And let's suppose your final choice narrows down to three houses: a brand new tract house, a probable bargain in a somewhat wilted looking older house, and an older house that has been made like new again.

120

What are your actual choices?

1. The new property with its attendant expense of settling in to your complete satisfaction.
2. A house about whose condition you are somewhat uncertain.
3. A house that is not new, but that feels like new, and that carries with it receipted bills and guarantees to show that it *is* like new.

Perhaps you, personally, would decide on either the new or the wilted looking property. The matter of personal preference and the matter of reaching for a profit through rehabilitation enter into this.

The great majority of your *customers,* however, will be strongly attracted to the trouble-free, less-costly-than-new property. All of the advantages of money saving, plus the advantages of known and established city neighborhood conveniences, enter into this.

Some customers will, of course, choose the new or the wilted. But *more* customers are looking for the plus value of the properly restored property. Such property puts them both money and comfort ahead. The professional rehabilitator knows this and profits accordingly.

● How to Fit List Price to Rehabilitation Needs

Today more than ever before you *need* an allowance for indicated restoration in your original listing price. This enables you or your buyer to profit on putting the property back in prime condition.

This very often means that you have to persuade your seller *at the outset* that he will be most *likely to sell* his property in terms of restoration. Moreover, he will sell at the best possible realistic price if *he* goes into the matter of restoration.

121

Most sellers do not realize the tempting alternative all buyers have: the possibility of claiming title to an *almost non-existent* equity in new property. They don't associate their problem with the fact that the biggest part of their possible 'market' is people saddled with heavy monthly commitments on cars, appliances, furniture, insurance programs, heavy income taxes, or some combination of these.

This large section of the potential market *cannot afford* the risk of heavy maintenance costs after making a strong down payment on a piece of real estate.

Are they poor credit risks? Not necessarily. They are often people with strong earning power and firm assets. But they are geared to new, guaranteed, theoretically trouble-free purchases. They are able to become possessors of a broad assortment of things *within their income*—so long as none of these things calls for more money than the original commitment. If the one-third-paid-for car breaks down, or the color TV stops working, *and the insurance doesn't cover it*, their whole purchasing program may falter.

It is no wonder, then, that they shy away from the uncertainties of much of the older property on the market.

Certainly a lot of customers have substantial cash and minimum debts to pay. They, too, are entitled to a sensible purchase price *in terms of repairs and replacements that will have to be made* to the property they buy. They, more than the debt-burdened buyer, are apt to demand it. The days of buying "a pig in a poke" are largely over!

For either kind of buyer you need to present a thoroughgoing, realistic understanding of both the advantages and the future items of expense each offering presents.

You have two choices. You can show them a property *that has been* restored to like-new condition, with the receipted bills, reports, and guarantees that prove it. Or you can show the property *in need of* restoration, priced along

122

with the estimates and suggestions that will render the property virtually trouble free.

In either case you have justification for your sale price, and the buyer knows exactly what he has to anticipate in ownership of the property.

In either case, the person who *handles* the restoration will profit!

Selling your seller on this idea is only as easy as you make it. In the old days I seldom got away from a listing session in less than two or three hours. My knowledge of the *approximate costs* of restoration was fairly extensive—as yours will be if you set out to make it so. This knowledge enabled me to predict, within very close limits, what the property would actually sell for. Studying the size of the property, its needs, and the costs hadn't taken very long. Arriving at a probable price seldom took over half an hour. But *selling the seller* takes time.

Most sellers are eager to know the marketing situation they are facing. Most of my sellers said that no one had ever taken the time to explain it to them.

The biggest thing they need to understand (at least some of them) is that a customer looks at a property *exactly as they would*. The customer shops. He sees a variety of possibilities at a variety of prices and payments required. He is often confused by what he sees. Price alone is not the criterion he thought it was. Quality enters into the value the customer will pay for. And most properties give only faint clues about their future, so far as the order of necessary expenditure goes. (Do you remember the John and Margaret story? I *told* them the house needed a new roof and approximately how much that would cost them. It was part of the restoration they were contemplating.)

In talking to your seller you need to convince him that a *good* real estate operator is as interested in satisfying the

123

buyer as he will be in satisfying the seller when it is his turn to buy.

Most sellers are willing to list their properties at a fair price once they understand what a fair price is. And what is a fair price? It's a price that won't *penalize* the buyer!

There is no reason in the world why you can't tell a seller the truth about his property. This usually has to be done very gently. Often the seller actually doesn't *see* his property as a stranger would—any more than he notices the wrinkles in the face of the wife he loves. It is often best accomplished by taking him out to see similar properties that *have* the elements of assurance that restoration brings about.

It always involves a breakdown of what is good and what is *uncertain* about the property he owns. It always calls for *eliminating the uncertainties!*

It is only common courtesy to really appreciate what is good about the property. You won't make the seller eager to resolve the uncertainties if you discount what he owns. *Praise* the lovely room, the view from this spot, the handiness of the location, or whatever it is, if it deserves praise. But get him to agree that you both had better *make sure* about the roof, or the plumbing, or the cost of a paint job, or whatever is needed in the arrival at a fair price.

Show *him* the possibility of profit through restoration. He may be just the person to make the property right and salable at an attractive price.

Show him what the *buyer* faces in the way of additional costs and *why* a buyer will want to fit this amount into a fair price for the "ready to go" property.

What is the formula for fitting listing price to needed restoration? It is a joint understanding of what he faces in selling and what the buyer faces in buying.

Bring about this common understanding on anticipating

needed restoration, and you will get a price and a property your buyer can take on with assurance.   You will get a real *selling* price—and both your buyer and your seller will know it is fair.

9.
CHANCES FOR PROFIT THAT DEVELOP FROM ADAPTABLE PROPERTY

BACK AT THE START OF CHAPTER 8 you read that practically every *bargain* property is subject to possible profit through adapting it to a new use or a new user.   This doesn't mean that a property *must* be a bargain before adaptation can be profitable.   It does mean that a person is more apt to add to, or subdivide, or alter a bargain property than he is to undertake such work on a property carrying today's full market price.   The high cost of adaptation takes care of that in most cases.

WHAT ADAPTATION MEANS

Now let's think about what adaptation means and about property that is adaptable.

One of the most familiar instances is the one you see in the magazines.   The old Spanish house is turned into a modern house by the elimination of arches, replacement of little windows with "let the outside in" windows, and so on. Another very familiar one is the "How We Added Another Room" story.   And another is the story, with diagram, of

126

snipping off a corner or side of the big bedroom to create a dressing room and bath.

The change to 'modern' is adaptation to a *style* trend. The extra room that is added on is adaptation to the *needs* of a user. The dressing room and bath is adaptation to more comfortable use.

Each individual property to which these things were done was adaptable to its own particular improvement.

It is quite possible that the Spanish house was ill suited to the easy addition of another room or the creation of a dressing room and bath. Or it is possible that it was adapted to all three changes if they were deemed necessary. This range of possibilities is true of the other properties as well.

FACTS THAT UNDERWRITE PROFIT-ABLE ADAPTATION

In looking for profit through adaptation, every property can wisely be studied. In considering a bargain property, its varied potential *should* be studied for adaptability.

A number of facts about today's living *demands* exploring the possibilities of older property. Prices are high. Families are larger. And times are prosperous. People expect and find luxury and comfort features in new property. They look for it, or for provision for achieving it, in older property.

Another fact is that we have come into an age of style consciousness. This is aided and abetted by the people who produce furniture, fittings, and appliances. It is pointed up by the rise in activity of the interior decorators and the tons of print that treat of the matter. Thus the nondescript property may need to become Modern or Early American, Ranch Type or Tudor, or whatever. (There's a book, *Realtor's Guide to Architecture,* by A. Rowden King,[1] that will help you identify and develop architectural styles.)   Keen study of the styles of *new* property is particularly rewarding.

The final fact is that a lot of people have the desire for a certain kind of property without sufficient money to swing it.   That's where rehabilitation comes in.

Many of your listings are adaptable to better use!   You already know this.   You are quick to agree with a customer that another bedroom *could* be added here or to say, "Sure, sure, it'd be a cinch to enlarge those windows," or that "The pipes for another bathroom are probably right *here,*" (because of an adjoining room's existing plumbing).

The only trouble is, the customer often has to suggest it first.   He, rather than you, had been looking for something he could adapt to his own personal use.

Sometimes you are able to jump in, belatedly, and *sell* the chance to profit through adaptation.   More often the fact that the adaptation *hadn't* previously occurred to you makes the customer mistrust his own 'hunch.'   He, after all, usually knows less about property than you do.   If it was really a good idea, you probably would have suggested it to begin with!

You will be ahead in sales, and your clientele will be ahead in both use and dollar value when you study possible adaptability *in advance*!

Adaptability covers a lot of territory.   We've spoken of adapting to a style trend, to the user's needs, and to more comfortable use.   Perhaps the most important adaptation of all is that of making a property *fit its surroundings.*

One of the most common 'bargain' properties we get to

---

[1] A. Rowden King, *Realtor's Guide to Architecture* (New York, Prentice-Hall, Inc., 1954).

128

sell is the property that is out of key with its neighbors: the structure that is smaller or cheaper looking or is the 'freak' in a block of otherwise conforming properties. It can be the old "dodo" that still stands in a new section or the single box-type house on a block built to gracefully slanted roofs.

Let adaptation rescue the freak or the misfit property!

When you are called on to list and sell the out-of-key property, you already have a handicap. Whatever the property's merits or faults, it isn't popular with the majority of buyers. The very fact of its being "different" even scares off many possible buyers who *recognize* its intrinsic worth.

The seller's real choice is usually between keeping his property or selling for far less than his neighbors' properties would bring. Often he, himself, bought it cheap, But now when he needs something different at today's higher prices, he can't *afford* to take a beating.

The preliminaries with such owners are always difficult. That first big plunge into what the property *will bring* is painful because both you and the seller know that it should bring more. If only . . . But you just have to knock off a good whopping amount because, frankly, people are not inclined to want this particular type of property in this location.

The seller is usually wise enough, if you make the necessary reasons clear, to offer the property at a bargain price. Unfortunately, even a bargain price may fail to move the property. A *lot* of the property that is rented year after year for less and less money as it becomes drabber and drabber is bargain property that simply doesn't sell when it is vacant.

The prospect of being "stuck" with a misfit property is

129

real. With the market apt to decline on older property that is *not* competitive, this is a possibility that should be included in your discussion of list price.

There has never been a time when it was more easy to get the funds necessary for wise adaptation.

There has never been a time when information, pictures, diagrams, effective corner-cutting materials, and means for definite *planning* of a wise adaptation have been so profusely offered.

If your seller undertakes the adaptation, he is very apt to recoup the value buried in the property. Moreover, he is considerably more apt to get a quick and easy sale at a fair price for property in his particular location.

If you and the seller accumulate and organize the information on the *easiest effective* adaptation of the property, you may even make an easy sale *without* doing the work! The profit-minded buyer can be convinced on the savings *he* will make by doing his own adaptation.

But even the man out *looking* for rehabilitation profit may not recognize this opportunity on the freak or misfit property unless you make it easy! This calls for thoroughgoing, all-out preparation of an action plan to *wipe out* the features that make the property "different."

Find out what it will cost and involve to put a slant roof on the flat top! Get an estimate on adding a room or a car port to the skimpy property! Find out what the least expensive way to rejuvenate the old dodo is!

Adaptation can rescue the freak or misfit property at the same time it smooths out the "quirk" in anotherwise consistent neighborhood. Sell it! Use it! Fit your list price around it!

You'll be glad you did.

130

● How Location Can Underwrite
Profitable Adaptation

One of the 'sleepers' we are all apt to overlook is the 'steal' in a grubby old neighborhood.

Your first information about it often comes from an owner's ad of it in the classified. You decide to run by it because the price sounds good. When you do run by it, you're disappointed. The price is OK you guess, but the property is in a poor, run-down section. It is forlorn looking. Probably wouldn't bring any more than that anyway. Maybe you list it. Maybe you don't.

With profitable rehabilitation up your sleeve, there is a good question you might get in the habit of asking yourself about such properties. The question is simple. "Is this 'steal' in a neighborhood that *should look* better?"

Think about the convenience of the location. Its accessibility to things people like to be near. Whether this is a neighborhood of owner-occupied property that *may* just be in a rut. Think whether there is some nearby attraction that lends use appeal and sales appeal.

Such a property *can* be the germ for a perfect epidemic of rehabilitation and renovation that will make all your selling in the area easier!

I'd like to pause, just briefly, on such a case.

I came to a greatly underpriced listing on an old street near a lovely little park. I saw to it that the property was beautifully refurbished, then resold it to a prideful owner. Soon the neighbors on either side and across the street started cleaning up their properties.

Another shabby property on the block came on the market. I met the owner and told him of the success that had

131

attended the neighboring refurbishing job.   He dressed his property up for sale.   I sold it.

The neighbors of the new owner got right to work brightening up their houses.   So far seven houses were refurbished.   One of these came up for sale, and I was asked to sell it.   I sold it overnight for a nice little profit.

The neighbor to its east had long wanted to sell his property.   He called me to ask what he should do.   I got him started on the right track by adding another bedroom.   He too made a profit when I sold his house.

Four more owners made their property nicer.

The next property that came on the market sold for almost *twice* what it would have six months before!   The neighbors began jokingly calling the street "Mary Street" when they learned that this higher priced property had actually merited 80 per cent FHA financing.

What started it?   Property that was *adapted* by way of its location to more enjoyable use!   That, plus a deliberate *push* in the direction of substantiating value that actually existed.   That *push* was the natural result often experienced by those of us who have given time and attention to rehabilitation.   A good 'start' in a neighborhood usually causes others to follow the example set by those who started the movement.

HOW TO VISUALIZE AND EFFECT POSSIBLE ADAPTATION OF STRUCTURE

I have dwelt at length on the long and thoughtful listing session.   This is the time when you and the owner can get together on your thinking.   It is also the time when you can orient yourself in the property.

When you are *in and on* property, you can pretend it is yours.   You can figure out what *you* would do to make it

132

better. You can listen to the *seller's* ideas on what could be done with the property. You can look at the window that might be cut into a door to a new room, look at the view that better windows might let in, measure the reason and the space for making this change and that. You can hazard a guess on what would have to be done to change the style, architecturally or fashionwise.

After you have left the property you can look into the actual mechanics of changing it this way or that. You can mentally envision whether it could be made to fit the buyer who wants *more* than the property represents as it stands. Or you can consult the builder or the architect who will know the best thing to do by way of adaptation.

Most important of all, you can listen to what your future customer wants. If the location and price of the property fit your customer *better* than those of properties that qualify as they stand, then you can sell *adaptation for profit*.

You can introduce the idea of developing what the customer wants from the perhaps unimpressive or even 'freak' property he sees. You can show him how he will actually get something for nothing if he undertakes the adaptation. In doing this you can very often bring about a change for the better in an entire neighborhood.

Your knowledge of adaptation possibilities is like a magnet. It attracts people who like to better themselves. It attracts the sellers of hard-to-sell properties that *often blossom into great value* after adaptation. It attracts the people who want to use their muscles and time instead of money in improving property. It attracts management of properties that you can adapt to a more satisfactory result or return.

Perhaps most exciting of all, it enables *you* to profit by adapting your own property to a new or better use.

10. CHANCES FOR PROFIT INHERENT TO USED INCOME PROPERTY

NOBODY KNOWS BETTER THAN THE real estate man or woman that income property is as individualistic as single residence property. An entire block may be built to identical income property units. Almost before the paint is dry some of them will show better income than others. By the time they are old income properties, the succession of owners and tenants will have carved an entirely different story in each unit—no matter how basically similar the units may be.

One owner may have been meticulous about maintenance and have good tenants. Another may try to be equally meticulous and have poor tenants. A building owned by a careless owner may be occupied by a quick turnover of good and poor tenants or, equally, by either good or bad tenants who stay a long, long time. The well maintained property may sell to an owner who 'milks' it. The rundown property may become the property of an owner who tries to improve it, either suddenly, or piecemeal.

More important, some owners and some tenants strive to keep up with, or ahead of, the times. Their property usu-

134

ally shows excellent income and sets a pace for less fortunate income property owners and users.

Let's stop a moment to think about keeping up with, or ahead of, the times. This doesn't mean just the obvious thing—the latest and best gadgets and accommodations, though these are vital to luxury income property. Instead it means *competing* with other parcels of income property of the same general kind.

In order to improve income you have to start with the people who will use it.

● How People Point the Way to Improved Income

If you are experienced in either rentals or property management, you can't help knowing one thing. Most tenants are comparison shoppers.

Even in the strong seller's market we've had for years, people have fought rent prices they considered too high. During that time they were powerless to demonstrate their very sound judgment of what rental accommodations were worth. If they had to rent, they usually had to pay the asking price.

Some tenants, of course, settle for less than others do. That is why we can come up with an *average* price for certain type accommodations, both in terms of the value of the property and in terms of the latest fluctuation in rent prices. There's never a time when a rental specialist or a property manager can't tell a prospective tenant just about what *average* price he will have to pay today for the kind of thing he wants.

That is our starting point in improving income through rehabilitation. Whether you are on a seller's or a buyer's market, people will pay a certain average price for any kind of rental unit. Your problem in improving income is one of two things: to bring the property *up to the average accommodations* for the price you want or to make the property *better than average to insure better than average rent* (or better than average tenants).

Your opinion of what is average or better than average is just one person's opinion. *The people who will rent* the rehabilitated property are the ones who determine the matter of average or better accommodations.

How do you read their minds in advance?

● How to Reach for the Best Possible Future Income

The rule for improving income property is the same whether you are about to improve the most luxurious apartment in town or to take the kinks out of Mrs. Murphy's boarding house.

You have to "make like a tenant."

You have to study that property as if you were about to move in on a three year lease. Why do you need to? Because that is what all the future tenants are going to do!

They're going to shop all the competition. They're going to find out what neighboring units supply and what neighboring tenants pay. They're going to see what other units have that these units do not have. They're going to compare notes with friends and with strangers!

They're very apt to follow the rental ads or the rental agents all over town to look at what their rent dollars will get them. And they're pretty sure to decide what they are willing to do *without* in order to save rent dollars.

Two eminently successful examples of improving income come to my mind—one the work of a couple of builders, the other the work of a wealthy investor.

The builder brothers bought a sadly rundown six-flat.

Grime and dirt were imbedded so deep you couldn't see what was underneath in the entranceway and stairwells. Loose wires, dangling and broken, provided single bulb lighting for the halls and stairways. One unit had been vacant for months (during the rental shortage), and the other five brought extremely low rentals, owing to their disreputable condition.

The first step was to get the tenants to stay during the renovation and to pay higher rent when their apartments were fixed up.

The next step was a vigorous cleanup. This brought the interior's good materials and construction back into view. For example, under the deep, entranceway grime they found fine quality marble.

The final step was *minimum* expenditure to correct the bad wiring, take care of leaks, and repaint throughout.

These efforts brought the net income up 19%!

The investor bought a delightful eight-unit apartment. His refurbishing was extensive—from installation of individual freezers and washers and a fancy recreation area to complete and expensive restyling of the entire interior. His efforts raised net income from six to 13 per cent!

Both of these projects started with the new owner "making like a tenant who wants to live *here*."

You can take this initial step on the income property listings you get. You *must* take it if you are to give sound advice toward profitable rehabilitation.

There is no blanket ruling for improving income, with the possible exception that people will usually choose clean property before dirty and enjoyable property before unpleasant.

Some income property calls for a complete overhaul and redirection. Some responds to a few spot changes. All benefit by better maintenance.

Your job is to find out certainly what people want in this

particular kind of property in this particular spot. The amount of rehabilitation than can be undertaken rests in what people will pay for the refurbished units.

You need to figure *in advance* whether the $2,000 worth of work this triplex calls for to make it competitive can be recovered within a reasonable time at reasonable rents. If it's going to take so long to pay off that $2,000 that *further* renovation will have to be undertaken before the original work is paid for, watch out! Even a thoughtless buyer can see that the effort would probably be unprofitable. He'll leave your average office and hie himself to a specialist in income property!

The spotting of potential profit through rehabilitating income property is *not* the private privilege of the income property broker. *You* can do it as well as he if you make the effort he does! If you're rusty on figuring income and expenses, *train yourself* or take a course and practice it until it is easy. Try it out on every used income property you list! Get the net return on this listing as it stands. Now try it out in terms of the better income that would accrue to the rehabilitation you've estimated.

You will be able to improve income through rehabilitation!

HOW TO IMPROVE YOUR OPERATION THROUGH INCOME DEVELOPMENT

One of the biggest selling problems we have to cope with on used and older properties is the terms they involve: Comparatively heavy monthly payments considering how much the buyer has paid down, because of the quicker maturity of the loan.

Add to this the fact that many buyers for older property are older people on reduced incomes and younger people who have not yet gotten into their earning stride. The problem of handling the monthly payments is often a stumbling block to buying an otherwise greatly wanted property, even when they can make the down payment.

Now let's take the seller's side of the picture. The seller often decides he must have a strong down payment because, from where *he* sits, the monthly payments will be so small. He *likes* the old couple or the young folks who want his property, but he's not quite sure they can actually swing the deal. He's half afraid he might have to take the property back a few years from now, and he wants to be done with it.

A device is needed whereby the payments are both easier for the buyer and reassuring to the seller.

We're always happy when we have modest income property to offer such buyers. And the seller is seldom worried about taking a comparatively low down payment when he knows there is income *from the property* that will help guarantee his payments.

● How Rehabilitation Eases Terms on Used Property in Income Zones

You already know how Mrs. Smith's little apartment in the rear of the lot behind her home is more than paying for itself.

It's old stuff to take in a roomer to help meet the payments.

And you've undoubtedly studied, more than once, the guest quarters developed in the attic, the garage or basement turned into living quarters, or the unneeded big bedroom equipped with bath and kitchenette to become an always rented 'single.' Maybe you've wondered about the pre-fab, mail order units you've read about.

139

These money making ideas are being created and developed every day. They always have been.

We're happy we can show properties that have these cushions of income for the owner to relax on.

Yet how often do we think to *install or develop* these or similar cushions in the heavy term, older property where they'd be so comfortable.

All the investment-built and public housing units in the world won't supplant the *decent*, lower priced rental in the familiar location where a tenant wants to stay. All the new construction everywhere won't attract a *lot* of people who either cannot or will not pay the tab for new property.

Don't let the fanfare about new construction cloud your vision. That construction is geared to the economy. A lot of people's incomes are not. That construction is, in large part, geared to the automobile. A lot of people do not own automobiles.

And don't confuse what I am talking about with the grubby, ugly abortive things people do to property in the name of income.

Decent, attractive, and *competitive* rentals can be achieved through *good* rehabilitation. Such rentals will attract not only the people who can't or won't pay for new rentals. They'll attract the people who *can*!

If you doubt this, go out and try to find yourself an appealing rental in older property. It will be the merest chance if you find even one. They're always occupied. And at good strong prices.

Way back over fifteen years ago I had occasion to sell a modest property that consisted of a nice little two bedroom house on the front and a dreary, grubby little house in the rear. The husband's income was not large. The rear unit brought $20 a month. The seller was not in position to make any improvements, but was willing to take a small down payment with heavy payments on the balance.

In a discussion of ways and means with my buyers I suggested that the little rear unit *could* be furnished and given some atmosphere. That got them started. It became a "Farm Cottage," complete with wagon wheel, flower boxes, rag rugs, lantern type fixtures, and "pump" (connected to the water pipe that skirted the front porch, on the front rail of which the "pump" rested), found at a second hand store. Grand total for furnishings (yes, a complete houseful of perfectly good furniture that didn't fit into an owner's new house) for just over $200. The decorating and fixing of the structure was minimal, but well done. As I recall, it came to about $150, including a little homemade rustic fence that set the unit apart.

My new owners described it when they advertised it without price. It was snapped up by an eager tenant, a professional woman, who offered $95 a month. It carried that $95 all through rent control. It is now bringing $135. The rental paid the entire property off long ago. There is still clean kalsomine on the walls. Through the years the owners have gradually replaced much of the original furniture with more interesting, more "farm like" bargain used furniture. And the pump still squirts water into the window box for the benefit of visitors.

An exaggerated stroke of luck? Probably. But any good renovation toward making the older rental unit *competitive with new* would have resulted in a considerable increase in what people thought it worth.

I'd hate to try to recall how many tenants and buyers came to our office looking for something "cute—like the Farmhouse"!

Out of that came South Sea garage apartments, "mountain" cabins, Chinese influence attic apartments, scads of 'Moderne,' and goodness knows what else—all at juicy rentals that made ownership possible.   Often, for example, in a duplex, the new buyer would fix the rental unit up *first*, letting the bonus rent gradually rehabilitate the other side, or other floor, where he lived.

THINK ABOUT sale terms that people can handle!   Installing income through rehabilitation of the properly zoned property can be a *key* to competitive terms!

Think about your seller's peace of mind when he carries a loan that is more than gilt edged.   (Wouldn't he love to take back that property.)   For that matter, think of the *price* you could get for him if *he* put his property in that kind of situation before selling!   At such a price he can well *afford* to take a small down payment!

And think about all the people who just can't figure out how to swing a purchase, even of the tired old property they'd settle for.

Maybe you and good rehabilitation can get them started!

As we said at the start of the chapter, you have to "make like a tenant for this property" to give sound advice.   Instead of a Farmhouse theme you may have to think of ramps instead of steps if this is an older people's neighborhood.   You may have to think of outdoor living, or unit kitchens, if they are what a tenant would pay well for here.

Whatever it is, *think* about it!   You'll do more business.

11. HOW TO DEVELOP CHANCES FOR PROFIT THROUGH CONVERSION

SOME OF THE MOST SPECTACULAR profits to rehabilitation come from the shrewd conversion of a property to an entirely different use.

A classic example is the Tea Shoppe made from an old barn. Another is the elegant professional suites made from an old house on a business street. Or there is the home made into income property. If you will look closely, you'll see an amazing number of properties functioning as something different from their original purpose.

The beauty in conversion profit compared with new building is that you start with an *existing adaptable* structure and location. Comparatively speaking, the cost of the "shell" for the new use is minimal. In terms of dollars and cents, you usually know in advance whether the location is really right for what you want to do.

WHAT YOU NEED TO KNOW IN ORDER TO PROFIT FROM CONVERSION

The real estate man or woman is in exceptionally fine position to spot conversion profit. By way of our everyday

143

work we are able at least to sense trends in our community. Through the deals we make we have at least an elementary knowledge of restrictions and zoning and construction standards. From contact we have more intimate and detailed knowledge of property than any of our clientele. And by observance we glimpse how conversion profit is achieved.

The weakness of the average operator is that he or she is willing to act without further information.

We notice, for instance, that a lot of people are moving into a certain area. We conclude that this is a good area and recommend it, generally speaking. We know that zoning exists, and we use general statements about restrictions, construction standards, and zoning to help us prove that a certain property is a good one. We take a certain interest in a conversion 'coup' that one of our clients achieves.

● You Need Specific Knowledge of the Property

To instigate or achieve conversion profit you need *more* than general knowledge. You need exact, specific, and comprehensive background information on the particular property under consideration.

One of the sorriest owners I know is a widow who bought a large house on the fringe of a beautiful residential district and made it into a rooming house. She fought for and got the necessary zoning, since the property was conceivably out of this prime area. What was her idea? She reasoned this way. There was a relative shortage of luxury accommodations for roomers in her town. Therefore if she *created* luxurious accommodations she would both get luxury rental for them and be able to live in fine

144

surroundings herself. Her idea was an excellent one.

How did it work out? Well, the neighborhood she selected was just one of those places where even rich roomers wouldn't think to look. The people who answered her ads found they had to take a bus or drive unusually far to get there. Moreover the property was just far enough from the heart of things that older, retired people would feel isolated.

What was even worse, the expensive house, plus the expensive type of remodeling it called for, forced her to try to charge prices she could not get. She had to take a job to support the property even after she found a few roomers at reduced rates.

Finally, she had no friends among the nice neighbors.

Her conversion of the property into a rooming house brought about a slight lessening of value to all the nearby property.

I don't know how she happened to buy that particular property or whether she sought advice on what she was doing. But I do know that she lacked enough information to make the conversion a real success.

● You Need to Know What to Avoid for Conversion Profit

Twenty million owners didn't spend one cent on their property last year. Another fifteen million spent an average of just $300.

There are a lot of things wrong with a lot of property.

Your common sense as a real estate man or woman labels *some* conversion undertakings as pure wishful thinking. The color picture magazines are full of Cinderalla stories of the magic transformations of which the owners are proud. A lot of these undertakings, if truth were told, cost

145

more than a reproduction of the final result *brand new*! And the barn-into-home or old-house-into-modern-home transformations account for the biggest volume of conversion by far!

We can appreciate these owners for enriching their lives and improving our selling territories. But in this book we are dealing with rehabilitation for profit. We want *our* clients to achieve the most result for the least expenditure.

Let's run through the most common precautions toward profit.

1. *Avoid an overelaborate undertaking!* Think about what the property *justifies*.
2. *Avoid UNECONOMIC structural changes!* Watch, from far off and from close inspection, for sagging, settling, warping. (An out-of-line window casing or door frame may be the clue.) A minor case can often be handled by simple jacking and ground level bracing. A major case, cured and long dried in that position, can cause unfeasible expense for correction.
3. *Avoid UNNECESSARY changes!* Use as much and as many sound parts of the structure as you can. The flourishes can be added later if funds permit.
4. *Avoid ASSUMING ANYTHING!* Find out about the wiring, the plumbing, the bracing, or whatever the problem is if you're not *sure*. The particular, probably newer, building code that affects *that* particular property may call for *extensive* changes. These may or may not be justified in terms of the total amount you have to spend.
   On the other hand, the old equipment may be *better* than you think. Unless you are adding more outlets or more plumbing fixtures or much heavier cabinetwork, or again, unless the code demands it, save here when you can!
5. *Avoid "make-do" when replacement is BETTER!*

146

> Maybe the old equipment for heavy use and duty *can* be repaired or repainted, and the old light fixtures and drawer pulls and switch plates cleaned up. NEW ones are *part* of modernization to create *new* value. They add salability worth many times their cost!

When you think ahead in terms of these common sense precautions, using your brains and five senses and borrowing those of the building trades people, you're NOT apt to undertake a topheavy venture!

I'm sure the widow, after rushing ahead on her hasty undertaking, would agree!

THE NECESSARY INGREDIENTS TO PROFITABLE CONVERSION

If you will keep the widow's story in mind you will grasp this quickly.

> 1. *There has to be a need for the conversion.* This need may be created by a shortage of such facilities in the community or in the neighborhood, or it could be a demand by a known group of people for something that doesn't exist.

Let's point out a few of the possible needs. The widow's idea of meeting the shortage of luxury rooming house accommodations was a good one. Another case might be a shortage of suitable office space in a given neighborhood. It might be the fact that a lot of substantial people in your town spend time and money in *another* nearby town enjoying its Little Theater. It might be that your town's crop of older citizens needing proper accommodations and care has suddenly increased. It might be the fact that a residential neighborhood is being forced to supply rental accommodations because of some new business or industry that has started up nearby. It could be that your town has a lot of eating places, but no outstandingly good places to eat. Or, in reverse, the kids may be driving for miles for a hamburger and juke box palace. It can be the need for either more chain stores or more independently run stores. It can be the need for starting points for small industry.

How do you substantiate such a need?

By using every facility at your command to put yourself in the place of the person who will make the investment in the conversion.

Talk to your Chamber of Commerce, your Better Business Bureau, to the Business (or whatever it is called) Licensing Department at your city hall, and to the local bankers or investment houses. They will have a long range point of view, based on other peoples' experiences, that is valuable in establishing need.

If such conversions have already been made, talk to the people who are living with the results—the original investor, the owner, the user. See how their cases worked out and what they'd do differently another time.

If your town presently lacks the thing you hope to create, talk to possible future *users* of that facility. Get *their* ideas on what they would like to have. Usually their combined ideas will define the need.

I can't resist suggesting one possibly foolhardy thing. I have seen cases, and so have you, where somebody started some utterly "screwy" new thing by means of property conversion. It was the sort of gamble that no conservative business man would either encourage or finance. Once in a while the supposedly "screwy" idea is a smash hit.

If you happen to become involved in providing the prop-

148

erty or the wherewithal, trust *your own* knowledge of your town and its people. Go after all the sound opinion you can muster, then weigh it against your own certainty. One of my customers started a *quail* raising business. He and the quail flourished, and the neighbors—if they happened to notice it—found it delightful!

Get your mind grooved to discovering and exploring *needs* in your town! They are the first requisite to profitable conversion.

2. *The neighborhood must be suitable to the conversion.*

This starts with permissive zoning or the certain knowledge that such zoning can be looked for in the near future. The Zoning Ordinance and the people who implement it can help you on this.

Conformity to a suitable neighborhood is the second important element. The widow implanted a conflicting use of property and paid a heavy penalty. This does not mean that you can't pioneer a new kind of use. You can, and must, to profit on conversion. It does mean that the neighborhood should be *made better,* in one way or another, by what is done. Start *good* conversion to income property in the old R-2 block that is built up to good, well kept homes. Make sure that the Little Theatre building you're creating out of an old market building or barn is in a spot where it can function (and provide ample parking) without inconveniencing anybody. Put the really good eating place in a structure that stands amidst other good and attractive establishments or isolate it completely from all local competition.

Make the conversion fit and improve its setting, and it will prosper.

149

3. *The kind of structure you end with must conform to the requirements of the Building Code.*

In changing a property from one use to another entirely different one, you can easily run into unnecessary expense and difficulty unless you "know the ropes." Be wise and remember that *prior* to any commitments on conversion *you should consult* with your Building or Engineering Department.

Find out ahead of time what has to be done, changed, strengthened, fireproofed, or whatever. It is part of your cost of conversion and something that *has* to be done anyway.

4. *The end result must be right for the new use.* This means that it is necessary *to think the whole thing through* in advance.

All too many conversions end in mild disappointment. The person with the original idea creates what *he thinks people want.* He sells his conversion opportunity short.

It is important, not only to think the project through, but to put it on paper so the eventual *users* of the property can think about it. Given this chance, they can often put the idea man back on the right track when he happens to be off it. You can help him get their ideas.

In a final analysis people 'go' for property with a valid attractiveness at a competitive price. If you want more return from the converted property, then you have to make it into something for which people will pay more.

HOW YOU CAN BRING ABOUT PROFIT THROUGH CONVERSION

You are in excellent position to combine the four ingredients to profitable conversion:

You can ferret out and verify the *needs* in your town.

You can find the spots where these needs can be met.

You can square the proposition away codewise, cost-wise, and profitwise and help your client attain either profit, complete satisfaction, or both.

You can guide the rehabilitator toward an enthusiastically appreciated end result, for himself or for the market.

12.
HOW TO INTEREST THE BUYER IN FIXING RUN-DOWN PROPERTY

IT'S ALL VERY WELL TO REALIZE that chances for rehabilitation profit exist. The thing that really interests you is how you are going to cash in on them.

These opportunities have been lying around for a long time. They were there yesterday, they're here today, and they'll be there tomorrow.

For that matter, they've surrounded all the brokers and salesmen of real estate everywhere—but only a handful of the brokers and salesmen have profited on rehabilitation either purposefully or inadvertently. So what's the catch?

There is a 'catch' of course. It's the same one that keeps the majority of real estate licensees away from real prosperity. It's the matter of how much you are willing to *put in* toward finding the right real estate for people and the right people for real estate.

THE THREE "EXTRAS" NEEDED FOR REHABILITATION PROFIT

A number of my fellow brokers have become quite intrigued with this book I'm writing. They're interested in

152

what I'm going to say. They hope I'm going to tell them something that will make them money, but they're not so sure I can. They run successful, or reasonably successful, offices, and it just doesn't seem probable that there is room for rehabilitation profit in a normal operation.

Do you know something? There really isn't room for rehabilitation in the "normal," average, lazy office.

Rehabilitation profit calls for three big extras: a lot more intimately-known listings, a lot more intimately known prospects, and a lot more individual work and thought.

FIRST EXTRA NEEDED IN YOUR OPERATION: MORE INTIMATELY KNOWN LISTINGS

Back on the coast of Maine, during some summers spent there when I was very young, I heard a saying that fits the 'catch' in rehabilitation profit. "Them that has, *gits!*"

If you *have* the live, thoroughgoing interest in people and property that you should have, you'll *git*.

You'll know so thoroughly the listings that interest you that you could appear on the "$64,000 Question" program on TV and go all the way to $64,000 on questions about that property. And you wouldn't have to go home a week to think over your next answer!

Now there's a catch in this, also. Most real estate people concentrate on getting a standard amount of knowledge about the properties everybody is working on. What's standard? Well, price, terms, number of bedrooms, number of baths, and whether the structure is frame, stucco, or brick—at least the front of it.

That's standard! If you doubt me, phone a dozen offices to inquire about an advertised property. Ask for the dimensions of the structure, the size of the living room, the brand name of furnace and water heater and how old they are, the age of the roof, and the taxes. Ask who the neighbors are and what they do for a living. Ask about TV reception. Ask about the floor covering in the kitchen, its color, pattern, and condition. If the windows are double hung or casement, inswinging, or out. Ask if the wiring, or even if the space, will handle your automatic washer, dryer, electric stove, and freezer.

Here's my prediction. One or two offices (or at least the person answering the phone) will click out most of the answers without a moment's hesitation. At least eight of the offices will give you a sales pitch on what a wonderful property it is, and promise to find out what you want to know and call you back. A couple will talk you down and insist that "you have to see this property to appreciate it." (Perhaps I'm being harsh on the willing-to-help-you eight offices. Some of them will tell you to wait a minute until they get out the listing card. From that they can often give you the lot size and taxes at least.)

Getting back to the subject, most real estate salesmen and brokers know a little something about most of the advertised properties. Some of them they know very well, having shown them or listed them. But it is likely that not one in a hundred brokers and salesmen knows a *lot* about everything that is advertised! They "mean to drop by and take a look," but they just don't happen to get around to it.

They set out to show a property on their listings that is being featured, and when the customer in the car asks about another house carrying a for-sale sign a block and a half away, the chances are good they'll "ad lib." If the customer is insistent on seeing this 'strange' property, do you know what often happens? OF COURSE YOU DO! The salesman knows that the customer wouldn't be interested in 'that' house. He understands they're asking way too much for it—that it takes a whale of a lot of cash to handle it. And by stepping on the gas and talking fast, the customer is safely past that house and at the door of the one the salesman intends to show.

How do I know this is true? Because once or twice in my early selling days I was tempted myself when I was *sure* that my listing fitted the customer to a T. But I know mostly because so many of my customers have been happily surprised when I showed them through a house they'd noticed, and found that it was *not* an over-priced, hard to handle property after all! Occasionally it was just what they wanted.

Suppose the salesman can't persuade his customer to forget the interesting stranger. Well, then there's nothing left to do but to bluff your way through. You arrive at the front door and ring the bell. Your heart is acting a little strange. You introduce yourself, tell the occupant that you "notice" that the property is for sale, and that you have a red hot prospect in the car. What's the price? May you show it? (The price sounds OK.)

Heartily, triumphantly, even jovially, you bring your customer to the door. If you're smart, you let the occupant map the course—so you don't accidentally say, "And this is the dining room," and run smack into a den or maid's room.

As you go through, you make a point of finding out about the existing loan and the taxes, so you can write it down when you get back to the office. Meanwhile steps are being taken, and everybody is sort of at loose ends. You see the house just about the same way the customer does and at the same time. Once in a while you find something to enthuse over. Usually within ten minutes you and the customer are back in the car, and you feel that you've satisfied the customer that you were right to begin with.

155

What am I trying to do, tell you how to show and sell property? No, not in this book.

I am trying to tell you that the listings that everybody works on are seldom listings that offer rehabilitation profit. *Occasionally* they are. And you have to know more than a little about every single featured property to separate the sheep from the goats.

● The Most Promising Property Is Usually Overlooked

The property that is most apt to show rehabilitation profit promise is usually a property that is overlooked by the other fellow. It may be the one he "means to drop by and see" that you *do* drop by and tie up quickly if it's any good for rehabilitation. It's the open listing you already have and remember because you know it so intimately. It's the property that lives, with all its details, in your mind until the rehabilitation profit opportunity asserts itself.

You're driving along, relaxing as much as safety permits, when all of a sudden you see that property in your mind's eye as if you were actually inside of it. Or maybe this happens as you're about to fall asleep at night or when you're sitting waiting for somebody who's supposed to come in at three. You know in detail what could be done with it.

It's the property, known to other real estate people or not, that by virtue of every single thing about it, fits a particular customer or fits the kind of customer who wants to improve property for personal pleasure or use or for money gain.

You can't have an *average* real estate man's knowledge

156

of current listings and expect to make any money on re-habilitation. It just isn't enough.

● Be Able to Prove Your Property Is More Promising

You can't carry and refer to a listing card covered with writing while you show a 'sleeper,' a "profit maker," or a potentially desirable home and hope to make your point!!

You can't show this property you've labelled a "good buy for rehabilitation" and be asleep to the prices and details and conditions of other nearby property that is for sale. How can you *prove* that your property is more promising?

When you are offering a property that must have money spent on it after the sale is over, you have to have the *opportunity* broken down into definite, provable parts.

You have to be able to say (at your desk, before either you or the customer have an opportunity for a quick, helpful look) that the minimum necessary work to make the property right, usable, or profitably salable is *this*.

These minimum repairs will cost approximately so many dollars. The property is worth its present price *because* . . . and here the customer is reassured by lot size, taxes, a logically arrived at valuation on the structure or structures, a provable expectable rental price on the property, and *specific* information about the comparable price and condition of other properties for sale in the area.

On the basis of *the facts you can show,* the rehabilitated property will bring, or will be worth, somewhere between this many dollars and that many dollars, depending on how much work the new owner decides to do and on the state of the market at time of sale.

157

SECOND EXTRA NEEDED IN YOUR OPERATION: MORE INTIMATELY KNOWN PROSPECTS

Put yourself in a customer's place. Your agent tells you about a property you can fix up and make some money on. You're busy when he phones, but you like the fellow, so you listen. It sounds pretty good.

Exactly where is the property? (Maybe he will tell you, maybe not.) What kind of neighborhood is it in? How are properties moving in that neighborhood? What's wrong with the place? Is it the sort of property you'd enjoy fooling with? Why does he think so? How much cash would it take to swing it? How much would you have to spend on it? Why? What kind of bathroom has it? What about the plumbing? Are the rooms of decent size? Is it a do-it-yourself kind of undertaking or would professional help be needed? How big is the lot? What's the zone—could you add another unit? How much are the taxes? What would the place rent for in case it didn't sell right away? Is the place well built? Would it take an FHA or a VA loan, either before or after renovation? If not, why not? If the prospect for profit is so good, why is he calling *you* about it?

These and a thousand other possible questions enter into whether you personally are going to be interested enough to look at that property.

You, the customer, may be a person who knows a great deal about real estate: an owner of, or investor in, a substantial amount of property. If you are, you *know* the details that are important to wise investment. If your *agent* can't satisfy you on these important details, then you can only conclude he's probably not much of a real estate man.

● Detailed Knowledge Insures Present and Future Business

You, the customer, may be like the vast majority of our customers: a person with little real knowledge of property value or real estate practices. If you are, you look to your agent for answers to everything you'd like to know concerning the property. If your agent can't answer your simple questions, how much weight can you place on his advice? Even one or two hazy, or "don't know" answers can nullify his prediction of a worthwhile undertaking.

You, as a customer, have lost respect for your agent, and he has lost your goodwill and has incidentally denied himself the inevitable string of future business that, you, a happy customer send his way.

Now when you, as a salesman are offering *run down* property to people who could probably buy new or prime property just as easily, you need *twice* the amount of intimate knowledge about your listing that you need on your regular sales.

To begin with, you need to be able to demonstrate the value of this particular *property* to be above anything similar your customer might see with another agent. He must be able to buy the same footage, the same desirability of neighborhood, the same pleasant use function, the same elements of construction here for considerably less money.

He needs to understand *why* the price of the property compensates for the needed work. He won't understand why unless you are able to equip him, when he asks, with facts on footage, neighborhood, and construction, plus details of potential use.

Second, he needs facts, which he can depend upon, on

what must be done to the property (if anything *must* be done). You need to be able to answer him fairly accurately if he wants to know how old the water heater is, how much it would cost to replace the kitchen linoleum, or the price of whatever he thinks should be done.

You need to know whether his suggestion of elaborate and extensive work is justified in terms of competitive offerings in the nearby area. And so you need to be pretty sure about the outside limits of sensible rehabilitation expenditure. This takes in intimate knowledge of the known competition, and in particular, nearby competition. You need to be able to discourage the buyer who, it turns out, just can't swing the whole operation. (You're neither able to see him through nor able to achieve your combined objective on an inadequate program.)

Only if you know *enough* about both the individual property and its logical improvement, can you sell the property that needs extensive work. Your customer will not profit on his work and expenditure if you, by default, encourage him to do the wrong thing.

So the first big extra effort most real estate men and women need to put forth is to know *more* properties *better*. The second is to know your customer. This is not a matter of becoming an encyclopaedia. It *is* a matter of equipping yourself, through concentrated and intelligent effort, to distinguish between the listings you can *afford* to get behind and the ones you can't, the customers you should support and the ones to discourage.

THIRD EXTRA NEEDED IN YOUR OPERATION: MORE INDIVIDUAL WORK AND THOUGHT

The hundred and one deciding details you know about your listings and their individual competition are simply *your private* yardstick for substantiating value and price.

Your customer (or your seller, for that matter) may be interested in all, some, or none of these items of information.

You presumably know all about property. Your seller or buyer knows something about property improvement. It would be hard to find anybody who hasn't at least been exposed to property improvement in one form or another.

I've heard brokers and salesmen, showing properties in need of work, go into floods, avalanches, barrages of talk on the peculiarities of the structure, the nature of the needed repairs, the case histories that prove how much they know about property improvement. And I've watched their customers creep back into a defensive shell.

● The Presentation That SELLS Run-down Property

Tell your customers only about the work that *must* be done if a new loan is involved or whether the structure will suffer further damage if certain work is overlooked. Tell him about these things the moment you've finished saying that this is a property that will respond to rehabilitation in a way that will increase its present value. Give him a close estimate on the minimum *necessary* work, as *you* have looked into the situation, or as the owner contemplates it.

Here is a property he'd be wise to inspect. This is what is wrong with it that *should* be taken care of to preserve or increase value or salability.

There! You've said it.

Now, if he still wants to look at the property, let him LOOK!

He can *see* what he thinks needs to be done. You can

161

be very sure he'll *ask* about anything he doesn't like or understand.

He will be thinking, and thinking hard, as he looks . . . if you let him. If you'll just keep quiet and *let* him!

When he's all through looking and all through thinking, he may or may not be willing to listen to *your* rehabilitation suggestions. As often as not, he's bursting with ideas he wants to *ask and tell you* about.

Let him tell you! Be able to answer *every* question. Maybe his ideas are more difficult of achievements than he imagines. Let the facts and ideas toward a more workable plan drop quietly into the conversation. If he likes the property, and glimpses its possibilities, he'll welcome them. If he doesn't particularly like the property, or if the amount of apparently needed work seems staggering (as it often does on first consideration), don't add to his retreat by ranting on and on about all the work that could be done!

You are selling *property*, not a repair program. You have made allowance for its condition in the price. This can be made a more appealing and more salable property. When it is, it will be worth more money.

The way you visualize improving the property may be a very excellent way. It may not be what the buyer will have in mind at all. If the buyer expects to move in and use that run down property you are recommending to him primarily as a *home* or a place for his business, then immediate use of the property rather than glamour is his chief interest. Don't forget that a lot of proud people have had to make their start in shabby property. If he is willing to use run down property in order to get a toehold of ownership in a piece of property, help him. It may take him weeks, or months, or years to make the place appealing.

● What the Buyers of Run-down
Property Will BUY

Your chief job is to establish the desirability of the property, its location, its size, its layout, the nearby attractions
or conveniences. *Your special and necessary responsibility* to the great majority of people who inspect run down
property is to build a foundation of value under the property *as it stands*! Unless you do, you'll find it rough sled-
ding to try to justify the often frightening first impression
of what has to be done.

Only intimate and extensive knowledge of everything
that may even possibly affect the property in question will
sell a value that more than compensates for the necessary
rehabilitation.

Does this mean that you can "take it easy" on the rehabilitation aspect of the property? Not at all! You may
be called on to figure out or implement half a dozen ways
to fix up the property. You very often will be called upon
to help the buyer borrow the money for the proposed work.
You usually will help arrange refinancing when he is ready
to sell the improved property.

Even the professional rehabilitator may turn to you for
advice and limitations on what he might do.

There is no substitute for knowing more than enough
about the property your customer is willing to see.

Knowing *something* about the property may enable you
to get a customer to look. Knowing quite a lot may enable
you to convince him of value.

But knowing the *one*, crazy, unimportant detail *he cares
about* can mean the difference between his being willing
to buy and to fix it up or his turning the proposition down.

Don't you hate to lose a sale for a *foolish* reason?

163

13. TRADE-IN: WHERE PROFITABLE REHABILITATION EARNED ITS SPURS

TRADE-IN, THE PROCESS BY WHICH one fellow trades what he doesn't want for something the other fellow doesn't want, probably goes as far back as the cave men.   It is one of the few ways in the world to get something you want with little or no money.   It prevents your being caught with more property than you can handle. (How often have you heard a buyer say: "It certainly *is* a wonderful property, BUT I wouldn't want to have two places on my hands"?)

Exchanging moves extremely hard to sell property.   It gains extremely nice property.   The reverse is also true. It also does commendable things toward reducing one's capital gains tax.

For all of these reasons it has been a favored practice with both canny investors and hungry property owners for a long, long time.   And astute real estate men, all along the way, have taught them much of what they know.

If you are one of the many who somehow mistrust trades (on the theory that one of the parties is usually *right* in wanting to get rid of what he has) I urge you to read a very enlightening book.   It is called *Profitable Real Estate*

164

Exchanging.[1] It will resolve any doubts you may have and point the way to a tremendously enriched operation.

Meanwhile, let's tie you and your office, rehabilitation, and trade-in all together. It's a glorious combination.

BELIEVE IT OR NOT, EVERY OFFICE HANDLES EXCHANGES!

Many highly successful operators do a brisk business in both hard-to-sell property and property you'd give your eye teeth to collect a commission on. They turn two or more properties in one operation, collect two or more commissions, and call it exchanging or trading.

All of us, whether we call ourselves traders or not, do most of our business for one simple reason. Somebody doesn't want what he now owns; he wants something different.

So we sell what he owns, and we find something belonging to somebody else that he wants. In this case it is a two stage transaction, with two commissions. "We don't trade," you'd say stiffly, if asked—bypassing the chance that the two *might* have wanted each other's property.

● A Case of "We Don't Trade" Exchanging

Most property owners are as initially disinterested in trading as most real estate people are. "You never know what you might get *into!*" is the usual way it is stated.

Yet there isn't an experienced broker anywhere who hasn't at one time or another worked on a perfectly good property that simply *would not* sell.

At long last somebody comes along who *wants* that prop-

---

[1] Richard R. Reno, *Profitable Real Estate Exchanging* (Englewood Cliffs, N. J.: Prentice-Hall, Inc., 1956).

erty. But he has to sell his own place first—and that may or may not be easy.

Your listing has expired or is about to.

You suddenly realize that the owner of your original listing *could,* perhaps, use this man's property. At least, if he didn't want to keep it, it would be a lot easier to sell than the one he now has.

To your unbound joy that owner says *yes,* he'll take that other property as part payment.

For a moment you're stopped. Does your state, or doesn't it, require an additional license to collect two commissions? You're in something of a dither about working out all the details. But you *do* work them out. And everybody is happy, especially you.

It's one of the "tough" deals you're proud of.

WHY PEOPLE ARE DOING MORE TRADING TODAY

We've said it before; let's say it again. Today's real estate picture and today's prices are different and better than yesterday's. A host of people do *not* know what their property is worth. To be on the safe side they set its value high. This makes both sale and financing difficult.

But these are prosperous days, and everybody who can find real estate that suits him better *wants* to acquire it.

Many people are served by real estate offices that have a struggle turning good but hard to sell property. These offices do a fine job of *trying* to sell the property. They spend money on advertising and time and effort on showing. But as often as not the non-competitive property remains unsold.

This same property traded on another property at similarly high-set value can provide both owners with something they like better. It's like trading a $5 potato for a

$5 beet. Suppose you either don't like potatoes or you don't like beets. Nobody will buy your particular vegetable. Then a trade is a dandy solution, providing you *do* like the other fellow's vegetable.

Part of the time one party to the trade does most genuinely *want* what the other fellow has.

Just as often he accepts what the other fellow has because he likes it *more* than he likes what he now owns. Any experienced trader will agree that it may take half a dozen swaps to arrive, through trading, at exactly what the person wanted when he first agreed to trade. This helps keep an exchange broker happy.

Once you've gotten the knack of trading, it's an incredibly lucrative business. Cash is secondary, but recoverable when you need it. Human understanding and service are paramount.

No, I'm not trying to sell you on exchanging, effective as it is in achieving what straight selling may not.

Rather, I'm suggesting that you may not be aware of the amount of trading that is going on today. Alert offices have long been cashing in on this often frowned-upon bonanza.

Today's economy encourages trading! People can be fully committed both cashwise and incomewise. But their property is regarded as security for generous financing *as it never has* been before!

A TRICK THE TRADER OFTEN MISSES

Many of the exchanges you read or hear about involve, on at least one side, a somewhat forlorn property. This forlorn property is usually the motivation for the trade. Its faults are the pivot on which the money aspects of the deal revolve.

Sometimes the owner of the forlorn property is pretty determined in his disregard for his property. He knows its every fault. He sees no possible virtue. "Get *rid* of the thing!" is his innermost thought.

He may *name* a high price, if only to salve his pride. But he will *deal* at a realistic figure. The fellow who owns the other side of the exchange can almost sit back and name his own terms.

The conscientious exchange broker, established firmly in the middle, will see to it that *both* parties come out all right dollarwise.

But here's the trick that even *he* often misses.

● The Story Most Exchangers Tell

In most recountings of an exchange you will hear this: "In order to make the deal, we took such and such a property and cashed it out as best we could."

Usually, you will find, trading works out all right. It calls for positive thinking. It is taking a calculated step in order to do what one wants to do.

The original owner of the forlorn property may have been *right* in wanting to get rid of his property with all possible speed. If he *is* right, then the other fellow is now 'stuck' with the selling problem.

When everything is figured out, he *did* deal at a price that absorbed any loss the new owner might expectedly take. Positive thinking also allowed for this contingency.

● The Story You Seldom Hear About Exchanging

Sometimes you don't hear the full story of a trade.

168

It's a provable fact that most people who *have* better property have that good property because they're pretty shrewd.

They like and appreciate property and its possibilities!

Instead of maintaining a mental block against the possibilities of a forlorn property (a condition lots of owners of forlorn property develop) smart people take time off to think. Maybe they take this time while the other fellow to the exchange is licking his chops in anticipation.

At any rate, they instantly recognize that, as it stands, the forlorn property isn't fit for a dog on today's buyers' market.

● A True Account of the "Short" End of an Exchange

One of my clients accepted a weatherbeaten, bedraggled, but substantial old two-story house. This stood on a very short lot in an old but convenient location. The valuation in trade was $6,000—considerably more than the run-down property would possibly cash out for.

The old house had halfheartedly been turned into three units. The best unit rented for $18 a month, the others for $15. I was elected to manage it.

Rehabilitation of the property, with a strong push toward modernization, cost approximately $3,000.

The best unit's rent jumped to an unsolicited $50. The other two units rented immediately for $45 each. $140 a month for the three. Expense on the property was virtually stopped for the next couple of years, allowing a maintenance reserve to be built up. Taxes continued on the old valuation.

A far cry from "cashed it out and did the best we could."

• A True Account of an Exchange Under Pressure

Let me say at once that the "pressure" was not mine. It was one of those unaccountable periods that happen now and then when property sales stand virtually still.

A number of our local builders found themselves with unsold new houses. One of them, formerly reluctant to deal with a broker, decided to give in and list his new house with us.

We really tried to sell that property! Here was a chance to get "in" with the builder! He built delightful structures.

A prominent and rising young businessman in town, a chap we had been working with on used property, looked at, and fell in love with, that new house.

Fate seemed against us all. He owned and occupied about the world's dullest old house. He'd have to sell that first. He knew things were slow. He also opined that things would pick up. They always do. In addition he knew to a penny what his property was worth. He'd honestly rather lose out on the new house than sell his old one at a sacrifice. That wasn't his idea of good business.

I took the young man over to meet the builder at the new house. (You know that yearning hope that just *one more look* might soften his heart!) They took to each other at once. The builder was flattered that this prominent man liked his house. The sad story came out. Both agreed to see what they could do.

My buyer had not 'softened,' he told me on the way back to his office.

That evening I went to the builder's home for a serious talk. I reminded him that my buyer had not questioned the price of his new house. Also that my buyer was of

170

sufficient prominence to make what he had suggested I offer a bit embarrassing to turn down. He wanted to use his old house as part payment.

I let the builder think a bit before I said any more. *He* knew that he couldn't go on building with his money and credit tied up in an unsold structure.

We both knew that the young man's house would be hard to sell as it stood. But since the builder was *not* busy, his men *could* get busy to make it more salable. If he would do as I suggested, I promised to see to it that he would have no problem there.

He didn't know old property, and he didn't like it, he said. But he would go with me to see it.

After we left the old house we discussed improvements that were needed for both salability and price enough to cover the costs. He reluctantly agreed to accept the old house as part payment. He *had* to get busy building again. But he was an unhappy man. Here he was, taking on an old place and preparing to spend a lot of money on it!

The young couple were elated and congratulated themselves and us on a fine deal.

The builder realized a profit of $600 net on the old house, which provided wages for his men—and *its* buyers got a bargain!

From that time on we were *that* builder's only agent. He never again hesitated to consider any deal of similar nature we could submit. He *liked* the bonus profit that the older property often offered.

LET'S STUDY THE LATEST PUBLIC WORD ON TRADE-IN

Perhaps you wonder why I've gone on talking about so much you already know about exchanging.

The following article appeared in the July 30, 1956 issue

of TIME Magazine. It is reprinted by permission; copyright Time, Inc. 1956.

TRADE-IN HOUSING

A BIG NEW MARKET FOR BUILDERS

Construction of private housing has been slipping in recent months, is now running at the annual rate of 1,100,000 starts, off 200,000 from last year. So far, builders are not too worried; the trend to bigger, more expensive houses has helped maintain a high dollar volume. Nevertheless, the decline has given a big boost to a little-known idea: trade-in housing. Detroit Builder-Broker Gordon Williamson, who used to sell cars in the '20s, says that real-estate dealers are today at the point where auto dealers found themselves 30 years ago; they are going to have to handle trade-in houses to stay in business, because "we're running out of first-home buyers right now." Agrees Federal Housing Administrator Norman Mason: trade-ins would open up "a great new market of perhaps 60 million Americans who would like to move if only they could sell the house they already own."

To spur trade-ins, FHA has put into effect a liberalized financing program. For the first time real-estate brokers and land developers are eligible for FHA mortgages on trade-in deals, thus freeing them of the financial burden of carrying trade-ins on their own. Furthermore, builders who take trade-ins are no longer required to make FHA-approved major improvements before reselling them. Builders complain that the FHA still takes too long to move, appraises houses too low, lends too little on mortgages. In most cases, builders can get a top of 85% on the owner's mortgage, which in turn represents a top of 86% of the FHA appraisal; *e.g.*, on a $10,000 house, the FHA trade-in mortgage loan insurance comes to about

172

$7,300. Yet despite these obstacles, trade-ins have been catching on.

•

In Detroit, where the idea is widespread, Edward Rose & Sons, one of the area's biggest builder-brokers, works this way: when the prospective house buyer cannot finance the deal until his old house is sold, Rose contracts to buy the house at a fair market price, puts it up for sale. If the old house is sold before the new one is ready, Rose simply charges the standard 5% broker's commission. Otherwise he moves the buyer into the new house and takes up his option on the trade-in at the mutually agreed price, less the 5% commission and a $750 flat fee for mortgage financing, necessary repairs and other contingencies. Out of 175 such houses handled, Rose has had to carry only a dozen past the new home transaction deadlines. Chicago's William Trude offers a trade-in customer 15% under market value for his old house, then gives him 90 days to sell it on his own. The customer usually succeeds, much to the delight of Trude, who has had to take over only four out of 150 trade-ins.

San Francisco's Standard Building Co., which has handled several thousand trade-in deals, sends appraisers to the prospective buyer's old house, tries to offer a fair market price. Once the deal goes through, Standard modernizes the trade-in, gives it a fresh coat of paint, then sells it. Standard expects little profit on the old house, makes its money on the new ones it sells.

•

But trade-in housing also has some handicaps. It requires considerable capital and is no place for small operators; a few slow deals can tie up their limited assets in vacant houses. Phoenix's Universal Homes averages ten trades a month, employs a 25-man crew to do nothing but clean and repair houses taken in trade. But when it started trading in 1952, it lost $25,000 the first year, before it learned that trades

173

require plenty of capital and a crack organization equipped to make expert appraisals and careful deals. Says President Whitney E. Anderson: "Without a separate organization for handling trade-ins, such as we now have, a builder could lose his shirt." Some builders set up a "trade-in partnership" with their salesmen. Each contributes a small sum (often taken from his trade-in commissions) to finance further trade-ins.

Another major trouble is the homeowner's inflated valuation of his home. Says veteran Cleveland Builder Joseph Siegler: "People think they have oil wells under their houses." Says an FHA official: "Most homeowners don't subtract the years they have lived in the house. No man selling a ten-year-old car expects to get anything like his original price out of it. Yet, though a house piles up mileage too and gets behind the times in style, the owner expects to sell for at least what he paid, and most expect a profit."

So far most builders, especially in areas where new houses are still selling well, are cool to trade-ins. But the trading idea is expected to spread fast as the housing boom falters. Family formations are already dropping sharply—895,000 new households in 1955 *v.* a whopping 1,650,000 in 1949. Says Seattle's William McPherson, who sells 200 houses a month, half involving trades: "The blush is off the first-time buyer. Builders are going to have to aim their selling at the trade-in market or go under."

There you have it. Still another approach to the millions of owners of used property who *used* to be considered the almost exclusive clientele of the real estate operator downtown.

A lot of people do go directly to the builder and his sales staff. But a lot of people do not.

A lot of you live and work in the vicinity of volume building. And all of you work close to the majority of builders

174

—builders who build one, two, or possibly a *few* more houses at a time.

Your established business deals primarily with people with substantial equities in good property. These people too are apt in today's growing exchange picture to become restless.

What is this going to mean? It means that if we cannot make satisfactory sale of their lesser property, they can still trade, with or without our assistance. It means, in time, that the owner of choice property—if sale is difficult —can copy the example of the builder. The idea will no longer be strange.

Most of them, of course, will follow the familiar pattern. They will come to you for the help you have always given.

TOMORROW'S SETUP FOR A PROSPEROUS OPERATION

Make no mistake about this. The enterprising real estate operator, the construction industry, and the government are all concerned with ennabling any property owner to become the owner of new property. A good volume of new construction is needed for replacement of property that finally becomes useless. A greater volume is needed to keep the wheels of our economy turning. And tomorrow's greater population establishes a base for action.

In the long view you wouldn't want it any other way. Your town and mine would not *have* the wealth of new development they now enjoy if these forces had not long ago joined hands.

People in our business are ready to implement this program. The people who are *prospering* on new construction today—and they are legion in our business across the country—reached this happy position through a sound decision. They rushed in to help their neighbors buy new

175

property and to help their local builders build what people would want.

Meanwhile the bulk of their possible competition have sat wryly by wondering: "How *can* you compete with 'nothing down'?"

These same prosperous and busy people already have a head start on trade-in business in the years ahead. They see the promise. Their selling territory benefits right along with their bank accounts.

The big real estate man and builder has *put* himself in position to reap the double advantage of sale of the new and the rehabilitation and sale of the older property. Why not? They've experimented. They're rolling.

The International Traders Club of the National Association of Real Estate Boards is a straw in the wind that you should observe. The group, starting in 1953, now has over 1,000 members. This number is perhaps insignificant unless you realize that there *is* a fee for belonging, and a member is not eligible to join unless he is *already a member* of the Brokers Institute! How many competitors in your town belong to the Brokers Institute of National?

These experienced exchangers, like the builders in the TIME magazine article, are ready to *handle any* hard to sell property!

Our clientele needs more fluidity. The 1950 U. S. Census figures showed that three fourths of our people live in urban areas. Studies of the use of land in our country demonstrate that all these people are concentrated on *two* per cent of our land. Real estate figures show 30 million of our people changing location (from home to home or place to place) each year. And only one real estate deal out of five is a move to new construction.

The people in our cities have been moving against tremendous pressure—with property that they *like* both hard to find and hard to buy. And the real estate man has shared their problem.

● Your Toehold on Tomorrow's Business: Profitable Rehabilitation

Only one thing aside from your ability to judge property wisely is going to *put* you in the running on tomorrow's business. That one thing is knowledge of and experience in rehabilitation *that pays off!*

You have a lot of people in your town with good older property and very little cash. You have a number of builders who cannot afford to hold an unsold property very long. And you have a lot of people with not new, but *choice*, property who are retarded from a move to other property. They have poured considerable money into their property over and above the property's ability to afford easy terms. Such property is the essence of the fine living that people are seeking, but it is both hard to sell and hard to buy.

Right now I feel something like the preacher must feel when he's *not* through with the sermon but the congregation IS!

THE PROBLEM ONLY YOU CAN SOLVE

The numerical majority of real estate people *can* fail to cash in on today's opportunity, just as they have missed out on offering the right *kind* of service to the building picture.

Only from now on the competition to yesterday's service will be stronger.

Trade-in and builder-handled rehabilitation does not

177

need you UNLESS YOU can make a better deal on each transaction that comes along than the trader or the builder can.

YOU start out with something that is invaluable to profit: an intimate knowledge of both how to SELL USED PROPERTY and of what the people in your town need and want and will pay for.

You can head off an exchange by enabling the older-property owner to make the *most* of his property prior to purchase of better property. You can't do this without offering the *extra* service of rehabilitation profit.

You can add profit and fluidity to an exchange.

Your local, casual-tempo operation is far superior to the volume builder's or the big time trader's set-up for making the *most* of each and every old property that comes along. But your ideal set-up for finding buyers for either "as is" or improved old property in the other fellow's deal has its own limitations.

Can you, individually, do a better job than they can? Your ability to *substantiate* a fair price is one that is peculiar to rehabilitation-minded salesmen.

You CAN sidestep the whole issue. Tomorrow's set-up on the sale of used property should be better than today's. You will have a lot of nearly new property to sell, as well as some lower priced property that has declined virtually to junk.

You can *become* more of a trader, more of a rehabilitator for profit, more of an *enabler* of the things people desire, or you can remain just as you are.

That's a problem only you can solve.

A POSTSCRIPT FOR REHABILITATION
CONVERTS ONLY

Perhaps your city, like mine, has grown to its limits. Wouldn't some of your oldtimers on choice lots downtown like to move out to the newer districts?

Perhaps you, as I have, have developed rehabilitator-investors who will buy old property to create new value and then *accept* run-down trade-ins on it. All they end up with is money.

14. DIRECT ROUTES TO ELI-GIBLE PROPERTY AND INTERESTED PROSPECTS

THE LONGEST WAY 'ROUND IS THE shortest way home.

There's a lot of good sense in that saying. It has helped me be patient a number of times—when every inch of red tape on a deal had to be unwound or when a seller or buyer had to unburden himself of a million accumulated words.

Often in the pressing demands of a busy day taking the "longest way 'round" was not only the shortest, but the ONLY way home to the idea or the deal that had to be put across.

You may have to take the longest way 'round on your start toward an operation enriched by profitable rehabilitation.

● Why Most Offices Are Not Already Profiting on Property Improvement

Most of the real estate people in this country work in a one-, two-, or three-man office. It's a logical way to

180

work. It cuts down on the quantity of promotion and advertising, on extra rent for extra space, and certainly on wear and tear on the broker who must try to provide a living for his staff. What's more, most communities simply don't provide the business for a number of large offices.

I'm certain I could ask you or any of your competitors why you don't know a great deal more about a great many properties and why you haven't already started cashing in on profitable rehabilitation—and get a typical answer.

You haven't *time*!

And I'd hate to step out of this little office this afternoon, without any recent preparation, to try to find a half dozen profit-making rehabilitation opportunities. It takes *time* to get in the groove of spotting good opportunities. And it takes time to build up a new clientele of rehabilitation-minded prospects.

Time seems to be the commodity we're all short on. Yet it usually works out that if you *let* things take their due and necessary time, you get the result you want with very little opposition.

Still, you haven't time. You'll keep in mind what you've read in this book, and if you happen to run across an eligible property or an interested prospect, you'll see what you can do.

Do you know something? *You haven't time to do that!*

Property rehabilitation is fast becoming one of the nation's biggest businesses. The up and coming real estate man or woman must *take* time or *make* time to prepare for getting on the bandwagon!

That's O.K. for some operators, you say, but *you can't* find time.

Rather than argue the point, I'm going to assume you're right and offer a rather simple means of extending and fortifying your operation.

181

THE SURE FIRE ROUTE TO MORE BUSINESS
THROUGH REHABILITATION

First, I'm going to say a word to the one man operation. It's a pretty nice way to work, isn't it? Whatever you make is yours. No office jealousy. No sales lost because of somebody's stupid blundering. Plenty of time to think things through. Low overhead.

• The Sure Fire Way to *Miss* Rehabilitation Profit

Have you ever thought of the people you can't serve? The ones who phone or come by while you're out of the office? The "little" people you can't afford to go out with, for fear of missing some "big" people?

Next I'm going to think back to my old, three-salesman office. None of these men 'had time' to serve all the people who needed help either.

Time for a coffee break? A haircut? To listen to the ball game? To read the paper?

Yes!

Time to talk . . . and talk . . . ?

Oh my, yes!

Time to go out with a 'hot' prospect or to inspect a prime listing?

Sure.

But no time for the people with whom I did *hundreds of thousands of dollars worth of business!* Month after month in those early depression days I made more money for my broker and myself handling "little" people than the two "big people" salesmen put together!

How many offices, even today, fail to realize that to-

182

day's BIG prospect may have only last year been what they'd consider "little."

● How to Start Building Your Operation Toward Rehabilitation Profit

There isn't an office in the land that can't offer one sales-man or rental woman the world with a string around it!

You'd probably have a hard time selling an old, experi-enced real estate man on what I'm about to suggest. The habits of years are hard to overcome. The idea of build-ing a time-consuming, broad, detailed, reinforced founda-tion under future prosperity usually doesn't appeal to the people who cut their teeth on the lush seller's market of the past few years. It's too slow. It starts too small.

But somewhere in your area there are a few 'green,' real estate licensees who are willing to *work hard* while they learn. They don't expect to make a killing right away. They've bought the idea that it takes time and experience to become competent. They'd be thrilled to try their wings under the auspices of a live, going office.

Give the *best* such new salesman or saleswoman (and by best, I mean the one you can't help liking because he or she is so open, so intelligent, so eager, so friendly, so sincere that *anybody* would like him or her) a desk, a phone, a stack of file cards, and some good advice.

Tell him to be the watchdog for your office. To greet with a whole-hearted welcome each and every person who drops in or phones while you are out.

Teach him to comb the streets and all the town's news-papers for possible rental listings. Tell him to drop in and get acquainted with owners of rental property, whether they're presently ready to pay a rental commission or not,

183

to appreciate their property, to make friends of them. This doesn't mean just the latest and best rental property. It means *any* property that has a vacancy.

Teach him to *study* every unit and every property he enters, to listen to what the owner or the present tenants have to say. Not only to listen, but to show a real and intelligent interest and to offer any possible help.

Teach him to make notes about property and to organize these notes for future reference.

It won't take a good beginner long to recognize values and proper attractions.

Offer this person's service to any of your own clients who may need rental help or service. Help him to do a good job, to learn about property management.

Start saving for *your own office's future business* the management business you may have neglected. Those little collection fees are a heavenly bonus to the beginner. Meanwhile, your office is growing closer and closer to the owner of that property who may later want to sell or to buy additional rental property.

Most important of all, insist that your beginner *try* to serve even the most seemingly impossible rental requests. It will start a chain of friendship that may last until today's "little" tenant becomes tomorrow's "bigger" tenant or buyer.

This trying to find the impossible rental is exactly the way to find property and prospects for profitable rehabilitation. *You* may feel that you have neither time nor the inclination for this type of business. Your beginner has.

Earmark the rehabilitation end of your office's services to your rental agent after he has become deeply immersed in the real problems of tenants and owners of not-for-sale properties!

184

HOW RENTALS DEVELOP BOTH MORE BUSINESS
AND REHABILITATION PROFIT

The real estate market is consistent in only one thing: it is constantly changing. Whether you personally are selling much property or not, people move about. Almost everybody at one time or another in his life *rents* rather than owns property.

Many, when times are lush, sell, intending to rent while they're looking for another place. Some, when times are slack, move into cheap rentals in order to keep up the payments on their more valuable property. (How often these people are confused, by one office after another, with "little" prospects!)

The newcomer in town usually *prefers* to rent while he orients himself in the new location! Wouldn't you? Yet how many of my competitors have *handed me* a sale prospect of a few months hence when they've told such a person, "Sorry, but our office doesn't handle rentals"!

To whom did they think those "little" people would turn when they were ready to buy? To the office whose policy denied them help when they really needed it? Or to the office that gave *equal attention* to the person who came in or phoned: "I'm looking for something to rent," as it gave to the individual who announced: "I'm looking for a place to buy!"

Even though many of those "rental" prospects didn't know I sold, as well as rented, property (after my broker had given me permission to do so) they always came back to my office and asked for me, when they were ready to buy! And that's all one needs when a customer *likes you* because of what you've done for him!

When young folks first marry they usually have to rent.

185

But that doesn't mean they plan a lifetime of inexpensive rentals!

Before very much time has passed *some* of those people your rental agent has served well are going to call on him to sell or manage their property or to find something for them to buy.

● How Know-How on Profitable Rehabilitation Develops Through Rentals

With rehabilitation that *pays off* up his sleeve, that beginner has the nucleus of a growing clientele.

You can well afford to *help* your beginner make an otherwise impossible sale of property *outside* the ranks of his experience. He, with any gumption and ambition at all, will be busy with the very real and prosaic problems of people and property. There will be momentous decisions of whether or not the owner can afford to redecorate the flat again or whether a good scrubbing will do. There will be exercise in figuring whether the sunporch *could* act as a nursery, providing the owner will allow a baby. There will be the *second* rental to an earlier rental prospect—this time usually to a much better place.

All along the way that rental activity revolves around the condition of property. That condition translates into dollars for rent. It finally translates into *profitable rehabilitation.*

It won't be long until you hear your rental salesman or saleswoman putting up a sound argument for paint and paper, or a cut in rent, or the reason *this* property is only worth such and such an amount in comparison with others.

And all along the way that rental or management activity provides *wider, deeper, more intimate contact with people* where they live, physically, mentally, and financially!

186

● The Bread and Butter Aspect of Rental Activity

Can you keep this beginner happy and eating on such a program? Maybe yes, maybe no. You may need to furnish a small salary for several months, balanced by the opportunity it gives you to get out of the office and among your clientele in the early hours of the day, before rental prospects usually come in. For instead of a casual receptionist, you'd have a budding real estate operator seeing each person that came in or making notes of the phone calls as a potential customer or client. And instead of a few noninformative phone numbers put down for your attention when you returned to the office, you'd have at least a little tangible information—by way of your novice's interest in a possible deal. (*Magic thought*, that, to a beginner!)

Undoubtedly, if your beginner has what it takes, there will come a time when he or she wants to begin selling. For a while that person can operate with feet in both camps—renting *and* selling. Maybe, eventually, you'll have to put him on full time as a salesman. All right, start again with a beginner that your new salesman can train. Your rental-trained salesman or saleswoman, you will soon find, will have a backlog of personal connections that the average operator working only on sales can't possibly have!

Meanwhile, you will share his or her knowledge of hitherto unexpected and unknown persons and properties. Just about everybody *wants* to own property. The rest may need to get rid of property.

Once your beginner knows enough to have the urge to sell as well as rent property, lend a hand! There need be no conflict. For years I handled *both* rentals and sales.

187

People who *wanted* my services would wait for me, whether wanting to rent or wanting to buy. At no time has your erstwhile beginner needed your whole-hearted support more than *now*.

Teach him how to take a good listing. Help develop sound *sale appraisal* habits and good selling techniques and procedures. Help provide property for the prospects whose needs he knows so well. And *protect* for a good and faithful worker every prospect and every property listing he has earned!

Few salespersons trained and treated in this way will be looking for greener pastures. You will have established for him such a pride in your office and depth of appreciation for you that no competitor can tempt them to leave you!

I don't know whether you glance at the rental ads in your local paper or papers. I always do. And the most interesting thing I've noted for the purpose of this book is that the rental columns get a little longer all the time. There was a time when my two-year old child's hand could cover the advertised vacancies. Not so now.

This holds a two-way promise for rental activity. First, there is once again on the present buyer's market an even chance that a 'rental agent' could make a living on rentals alone. Second, and more important, the increasing number of vacancies means just one thing: tougher competition for the older rental property.

In the not too distant future it will be *necessary* to rehabilitate and modernize much rental property or take a rather severe cut in rent. You, your office, and your rental agent can help *spike* that expected drop in the rental price for behind-the-times property in your own locality. In doing it you can win the loyalty of many discouraged

188

owners. In doing it well you can win the loyalty of the bargain-seeking tenant.

Recent surveys on a nationwide scale show that prices for new property are apt to rise for a while. Prices for property under ten years old remain strong. But prices for older property show a steady decline.

Shall we stand by and watch this intensify? Or shall we do our favored part as real estate operators in reestablishing competitive value in the older properties?

Who, *better* than the salesman specializing in rentals and, in the course of time, property management, experienced in what rehabilitation of property *can do* for both property and people, can help stem the tide of future decline?

You, the selling salesman, and you, the operating broker, can, of course, when you back up or emulate the activities of your office's rental agent.

● The Two-way Need for Expanding Your Service

The Real Estate office that gives equal attention to both selling and renting (So few offices do that now!) has a far better chance of profiting through rehabilitation than does the office which confines itself to sales alone!

Most owners will make the necessary effort and spend the necessary money. They will, that is, if somebody clears their vision and helps them *get* more income from property made more valuable through practical and forward looking revitalization.

Most tenants are eager to find comparatively quiet, comparatively more commodious, and definitely more accessible rentals.

The almost irrresistible attraction to new income property loses its potency if or when that new property loses its newness and develops the same old familiar headaches *in less elbow room!* And certainly older rental property gains in appeal when it offers competing charms for less money.

Neither you nor your rental agent can help the owner of an income property increase his rents (or at least hold the line on price) without becoming fairly intimately acquainted with that owner, his property, and its competition.

Nor can you promote and follow through a rehabilitation job on the not-for-sale property without learning something that will *help you sell* run down property!

Rental and management activity offer about as extensive a hold with a future prospect and a future "We want *you* to have the exclusive listing!" as you can possibly get.

These people know and appreciate you. You know and appreciate both them and their property. It's an unbeatable combination in a dog-eat-dog competitive business.

FREEWAY TO MORE INTIMATELY KNOWN PROSPECTS

The freeway to knowing more prospects more intimately is to cause *them* to want to know *you*.

Most successful offices know this and spend the most they can possibly afford to advertise what fine people they are. The trouble is—a lot of people don't read the classified columns.

There is NO substitute for personal, working *service* to all sorts of people. If you know the shoemaker who did a wonderful job on your old shoes, you're not apt to look in the yellow pages in the phone book for a shoe repair man.

But there IS a way to broadcast and intensify the impression that yours is a good office to do business with—to

190

show people that YOU are the person to see about profitable rehabilitation.

It starts, as all business does, with people.

● How to Become a Better-Known Real Estate Operator

Advertising is fine, but it is, after all, second-hand. Your office may be grand. But it is, after all, just one of a number of offices.

The person who doesn't *know* you will patronize the office about which he has heard something favorable or, knowing nothing about any of the offices, is most likely to choose the one that looks the best to him.

What can *you* do to become known as "the person to see" about nice property and profitable rehabilitation?

There are three things you can do.

1. You can make *your* office look alive, fresh, and competitive. Charity starts at home. So should rehabilitation. Get *rid* of the dust of ages, the clutter, the down-at-the-heel appearance.
2. You can start being a full time citizen. Who are the *well* known real estate people in your town? If you'll get a line on them, you'll find they're the people who are *interested* and *active* in a lot of things besides real estate. They get out and around in their expanding community. They see, and are seen by, lots of people.

They can be found at large meetings for this worthy cause or that. You will find them at their local PTA meeting or at church on Sunday. And you're very apt to find them at the graduation exercises of last year's customer's son—or at the wedding or funeral or public appearance of a friendly client.

191

You will very often find them in public service, in sports groups, in social groups, and in politics. They know what is going on "in the valley," "below the tracks," "across the line," and "at City Hall."

Is this a tongue in cheek activity? No!

They are taking their full place as responsible real estate operators in the *community* picture. They work at and enjoy being informed and useful citizens. And it pays off.

They become respected *familiar* people who make a living at real estate. The things they say about real estate, if the occasion presents itself, are listened to with interest because they are *people you know*.

3. You can identify yourself with property rehabilitation. Have you, personally, read about and investigated the program and accomplishments of the *American Council to Improve our Neighborhoods* (ACTION)? Do you know, personally, the merchants and contractors who are implementing *Operation Home Improvement* (OHI)? Have you talked to them and told them you want to help *your* clients improve their property?

Have you gone to your bank and your lending institutions and discussed financing for rehabilitation?

Have you gone to *see* some of these do-it-yourself or deluxe jobs some of your clients have done or are now doing on their properties?

• How to Become the "Person to See" About Rehabilitation

If you will bestir yourself to *become* a better known real estate man or woman who *knows* about profitable rehabilitation, the rest is ridiculously easy.

No matter where you go, out and around and busy in your community, you will find opportunities to mention the amazing and wonderful things that happen to people and property through wise rehabilitation.

And do you know something? The moment you do, everybody is *with* you! With all the tremendous advertising and promotion on *property improvement,* it's a fascinating subject!

You'll hardly be through telling how you or your rehabilitation specialist has achieved a triumph or how some anonymous buyer or seller has made a perfect dream place out of a shabby old barn when *everybody* wants to chime in.

They know of a drab property that could stand that sort of treatment. They have a nephew who is fixing up his place. They would like to find something like that to work on in their spare time. Or, *they* believe it's really cheaper to buy new. (And isn't *that* a juicy opening to help them buy something new or to help them make what they have *like* new so they can!)

If you'll stop to think a minute, *you* are interested in what the familiar and well known figure in the medical or automotive world around you has to say about the people and projects involved in his activities. You are *interested* in the information this professional may drop when he's talking.

If what he says makes *sense*—if it sounds good to you—you spot him as the *person to see* about your future medical or automobile needs or problems.

If you'll think a bit further, the people *working at* property rehabilitation are looking for a champion in the real estate field. If you *show* your interest in becoming adept at implementing OHI and ACTION—if you *know* how your client must have gone about his particular improvement project—then you are already identified with rehabilitation to a certain extent.

Your fellow club members, fellow workers in a cause,

your friends and clients, and your fellow participants in property rehabilitation *are* interested!

When you, a familiar and respected real estate man or woman, make *sense* on more enjoyable and better use of property—when you can explain and demonstrate *new value* in old property—then you BECOME the person to see for personal pleasure or money gain through rehabilitation. You have a recognizable value to the "big" prospect within range of your voice, as well as to the "little" prospect who didn't know such help was available.

They WANT to do business with YOU!

What more could you ask?

INDEX

INDEX

INDEX